Dr. Misner

Thank you 1
posting my book
your page on launch date
It did make #1!

Enjoy the read.
Best, Michael
Coach

M000190003

KNOCK IT OUT OF THE PARK LEADERSHIP

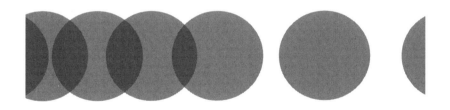

THE ABC'S OF ENTREPRENEURIAL SUCCESS

MICHAEL DILL

Knock It Out of the Park Leadership

First published in 2021 by

Panoma Press Ltd
48 St Vincent Drive, St Albans, Herts, AL1 5SJ, UK
info@panomapress.com
www.panomapress.com

Book layout by Neil Coe.

978-1-784529-51-2

DEDICATION

This book is dedicated to all those who strive to become their absolute best.

WHAT THEY'RE SAYING ABOUT *KNOCK IT OUT OF THE PARK LEADERSHIP*

"Short, sharp, and to the point is the best way to describe *Knock It Out of the Park Leadership*. Coach Michael lays out the proper ingredients in an easy-to-read format that if followed and applied will change your business and life. A must-read for any leader who wants to build an organization that works for them."

Brad Sugars
CEO & Founder
ActionCOACH

"Coach Michael is inspiring. He is all about attitude, action, and results. His lessons are timeless, and if you follow his advice, your business will thrive, your life will be filled with bliss, and your self-awareness and confidence will soar."

Pegine
Hall of Fame Speaker
Women Business Entrepreneur of the Year

"*Knock It Out of the Park Leadership* is a great foundation for anyone looking to better themselves or their organization. Michael's A, B, C approach to tackling many of the assets needed to succeed is refreshing and makes for an easy read. Highly recommend!"

Andy Cagnetta
CEO
Transworld Business Advisors

"Winning, overcoming, and leading doesn't happen on accident. Coach Michael lays out the purposeful path to confidence through preparation."

Brian Mast
U.S. Army Veteran, U.S. Congressman

"As easy as learning your ABC's and just as important, *Knock It Out of the Park Leadership* outlines the building blocks of successful leadership qualities in a way that teaches new leaders how to thrive while inspiring seasoned leaders to sharpen their skills. The author's personal testimonies make you feel like you're getting a one-on-one coaching session and his ability to set principles in real life context makes this book practical, and thoroughly enjoyable."

Jenni Morejon
President & CEO
Fort Lauderdale Downtown Development Authority

ACKNOWLEDGMENTS

As we all journey through our life of all our failures and successes at some point, we realize that we were never on this journey alone. We actually become a culmination of all the people, lessons, experiences, ups, downs, wins, and failures from this traveled path.

I would like to start by thanking Anthony Robbins as I took his Personal Power 30-Day program back in 1990 that set me on my path of personal self-improvement. Brian Tracey's *The Psychology of Winning* is the first self-improvement book that I read and read many times over. I would also like to thank all those who were part of this journey, those who have mentored me along the way. Those I've met at conferences, workshops, success seminars, including the books, podcasts, videos all being part of who I am today.

I want to pay special thanks to Brad Sugars and The ActionCOACH Organization for providing a vehicle for not only me, however, for so many to grow both personally and professionally while impacting thousands around the globe. This has been and continues to be an impactful, fulfilling, and glorious ride.

I owe deep gratitude to my parents who taught me if I wanted something bad enough to work hard and get it. I love and miss you both.

I would like to extend a proud sense of gratitude to both Victoria and Zachary, my two beautiful children who blessed me with the opportunity to be your loving father.

I would like to especially thank my wife Susan for sticking by me and being my number one fan through all the highs and lows that we have experienced together throughout our life.

I want to thank all my clients, past, present, and future for providing me an opportunity to be an impact on their businesses, teams, and lives.

I most importantly owe my deepest gratitude to God for first being patient in me finding you and truly having my back in guiding me through this journey of life and fulfillment.

PREFACE

"I don't know any other way to lead but by example."

Don Shula, Winningest NFL Coach

We have all heard the phrase that "knowledge is power!" I believe that this statement is actually slightly incorrect. I believe based on my experience that the "application of the knowledge is power."

We have all read books, listened to podcasts, attended events, lectures, speaking engagements, and/or conferences. We have highlighted words, lines, and paragraphs in books, dog-eared pages never to go back and look at them again. We have attended events and conferences where we took loads of notes with good intentions to go back and apply. However, most of those notes only ended up collecting dust.

Think about it, how many compositions or spiral notebooks do you have somewhere in your office or home that contain great ideas that have never been applied? Just to let you know, guilty as charged!

I had a mentor of mine years back ask me a couple of questions about a book I read numerous times. Unfortunately, I couldn't properly answer either one of the questions. Talk about a wake-up call.

The book was *Think and Grow Rich* written in 1937 by Napoleon Hill. I have since read that book the way it was originally intended to be read based on the principles in the book. When I finally understood the principles of the book, only then was I able to apply them in my own business and life as well as educate others on the same.

My message is to simply be intentional with your learnings. Create a learning log to record your notes and also how you are going to apply those learnings into your life and business. Take a day to fully debrief your notes after a conference, or better yet debrief with a partner while comparing notes. Write down what actions you are going to take, and most importantly, take one action immediately to create the intended momentum.

I have created this book with the intent to keep things simple with lessons we can understand and apply in both business and life. I have used a format of the ABC's as a tool to highlight different areas and lessons that if you properly practice and apply them, you will be able to build yourself up as a leader in addition to developing organizational strength.

When you incorporate the concepts and lessons of *Knock It Out of the Park Leadership* into your organization, you will experience increases in clarity, confidence, communication, ownership, leadership, retention, productivity, revenues, margins, and profits. Enjoy the journey.

CONTENTS

INTRODUCTION

"You must travel your own journey at your own pace; do not rush the process…

or assume that you have to accept someone else's choices for your life."

Thomas L. Jackson, Ph.D.

I believe our entire life becomes a series of moments stacked one on top of another in time that has a distinct impact on the direction of our lives. We all experience certain hardships that we have to get through that mold us, sometimes alone, sometimes with the help of others. These experiences and adversities actually strengthen and shine us up for the long haul in life. There are victories along the way both big and small that shape our confidence and serve us well on our journey.

I would like to think that our ultimate goal is to live a life of freedom, and independence. To actually feel comfortable in just being who we are. To take advantage of what we are presented on this earth while serving the greater good and having a positive impact on others.

This book is all about you – your self-awareness, expectations, emotions, efforts, and experiences and how it all impacts your success as well as others in both business and life.

There are many different moving parts and experiences that shape us on our journey through life, leadership, and business – with your permission, let me share mine.

It was April 30, 2012, my wife's birthday, that I received news that I was laid off from my six-and-a-half-year consulting position out of a firm in Pennsylvania. Not because I didn't perform, however, but because the company hit some rough spots, I was the furthest away and least likely to control so I was the first to go. I now fully realized that even though I was the top producer in the organization, I still was unable to control my ultimate outcome. I always felt I was running a business within a business, had control of my income based on my attitude, effort, and results; however, even though I somewhat wrote my own paycheck, I never actually signed my own paycheck. It was time for me to make a decision. It was time for me to take control of my ultimate outcome.

Doing my due diligence in the consideration of buying a coaching practice, with the understanding of this being a big decision, I didn't want to force it. I needed to go through the process to have the answer come to me.

Part of my process is to take a walk and let the correct decision materialize. It was a Saturday morning, somewhere in May. As I began my walk, I started to ask myself a series of questions. Going through this process, I walked across the main street, took one step up on to the curb on the other side and the first thing I saw was a statue of Mother Mary in front of a church.

At that very point, all bets were off and someone else was suddenly in charge. There's a line, "When the student is ready the teacher will appear." I can't tell you how much that phrase resonated with me that day. I began to experience sweats, chills, I was alternately shaking, laughing, crying, it was a total uncontrolled out of body experience. Before this moment if anyone was to share something even close to this type of experience, I simply wouldn't believe them.

I continued on with my walk somehow trying to get ahold of what just happened. After about 40 minutes of walking and filtering through the experience, I was finally back to feeling somewhat normal again. It was now time for me to walk back across the road to my complex. I took one step down off the curb, stopped, however, realizing I couldn't ignore what had just happened, I decided to embrace the moment, turn back around, and approached the statue of Mother Mary. I put my right hand on the head of the statue, looked up, and said, "I wasn't looking for a sign, however, if this is it, I will follow your lead and serve."

I realized at that moment that I was summoned to serve business owners to get the best out of themselves, their team, and their business. It was to have them see more in themselves than they thought was possible. To have the confidence to take the action to get them what they really wanted both in business and in life. I knew if I followed this sign and served in this manner, I would be creating a win/win for all involved.

I also knew being appointed to this position that it was time for me to step up to take on this role. It was time for me to put in the work to become my absolute very best. It was no longer about me anymore, I was here to serve.

It's amazing as I looked back and put everything into perspective. When I was perplexed in searching for the right direction, after 54 years in this life when it was time for me to really ante up, it was then at that moment that I received the tap on the shoulder. When we experience something like this, we have a choice to embrace it or not. I chose to embrace the sign.

As I look back at my life, I now understand that everything that has happened along my path has prepared me for that moment. Simply a 62-year+ journey on learning what it takes to be a leader to serve.

I believe that leadership is all about taking 100% ownership of oneself, no matter what the circumstances and surrounding occurrences. That sense of ownership raises us up to be a beacon of light to shine on others. I also now fully understand that wealth creation is a by-product of getting everyone else what they want, and when you show up and serve in this manner, everybody wins.

I would like to imagine that many of us truly want success, many of us dream of success, however, only those who do the work earn the right to have true success. I believe that my journey of 62+ years has not only provided me a much fuller and richer life, it has also earned me the right to serve as "The Master of Knock It Out of the Park Leadership."

CHAPTER 1:

IT'S ALL ABOUT ATTITUDE

"Ability is what you're capable of doing.
Motivation determines what you do.
Attitude determines how well you do it."

Lou Holtz, Former Football Player and Coach

A is the first letter of the alphabet for a reason as it's the first step of any successful endeavor. Whether it be in business or in life, the beginning always starts with a positive mental attitude.

A positive attitude is like a ripple in the water that causes a chain reaction of positive thoughts, events, and outcomes. It is a catalyst – a spark that creates extraordinary results.

In business and/or in life, you will most definitely experience some adversity along the way. You may be experiencing some right now. We've all been there. However, it is not what happens in life that matters; it is how you react to that adversity that really makes the difference. That difference is usually the result of what type of attitude you bring to that circumstance or event.

In business, attitude is extremely important especially if you are the owner or leader of an organization. It is your attitude that will filter down into the entire team. You are like a magnet that will either lift or lower the spirits of everyone else in the organization.

I think of times like the dot-com bust of 2000, the banking/ real estate collapse of 2008, and the extra-unusual year of 2020. We were all experiencing similar circumstances and realities. However, it was those who walked with a strong, confident attitude, an almost scary calm that automatically filtered down to their team, their clients, and everyone else they came in contact with, that, in many cases, was the difference between some companies either thriving or going bust.

Serving in the financial industry for 25 years and somewhat possessing an understanding of the boom/bust history of the market, I was venturing into the year of 2020 with the feeling that the financial market could be due for some rockiness. I actually acknowledged it on my SWOT (Strengths - Weakness - Opportunities - Threats) on my yearly plan under threats. I wrote "Economy: Don't let the outside affect the inside!" What I meant in writing that was in the understanding if 2020 was to get rocky, I was preconditioning myself to not let it affect my mindset or business in a negative way.

When the year slowly came unglued in March and continued on throughout the year, my clients and I were already in the "up our game mindset" that set the pace for our entire year. I'm happy, grateful, and proud that my clients and I fared fairly well through all the noise and controversy. I'm convinced that it was my original attitude that filtered down to my clients that kept us all positively in the game.

It is always in your attitude where you lift yourself up as well as others around you. There is an example, a great athlete as well as a great man that the world, unfortunately, lost on January 26, 2020. This man exhibited all the right principles; Kobe Bryant always brought the right attitude to the equation. You knew if you were a basketball player playing against Kobe Bryant, you better bring your "A" game or he was going to absolutely smoke you on the court.

Kobe had a great attitude. He had his serious face, his game face, and that cheerful smile when he was with the ones he loved. Kobe Bryant did the work, he worked hard on his game and on being his best. There are many great players that felt they had a great work ethic; however, when they compared to Kobe, they felt that they weren't even in the same level of work ethic. Because Kobe consistently exhibited the combination of a great attitude along with a strong work ethic, he produced extraordinary results.

What's the most interesting in Kobe's story is when you really show up in life and work with a great attitude, put in the effort, take the right action, while helping others along the way, you simply produce extraordinary results. With his example of excellence Kobe Bryant actually created a legacy for which he is honored and known worldwide.

Understand that your attitude is contagious, since anyone who really matters wants to do business with a winner. Condition yourself to carry an attitude of confidence and calm as that alone could be the winning combination to a thriving organization. In addition, let me share a little formula to remember: *Positive Mental Attitude = Pays More Always*. In business, since it always ends with the bottom line, that's just the proper formula of success you strive for.

Slow down for a moment and take inventory of yourself. Where do you need to shine up your attitude? What are some of the things you need to put in place? Write it down, create a plan, take action, follow through, stay in shape, physically and mentally, and I guarantee you'll get the results you're looking for.

In order to continue developing this positive attitude type culture and keep it filtering down to your team, you must ask yourself this question:

DO YOU HAVE SOLID ORGANIZATIONAL BENCH STRENGTH?

In any organization or sports team, any sustainable success will always come down to their bench strength. You've seen it in basketball games where the second-teamers would come off the bench and pull ahead in the score by outperforming the bench of the opposing team. We've seen it in football games when a first stringer would get injured and his back-up would come off the bench and perform successfully.

Bench strength in an organization is defined by the competence and number of employees who are ready to fill vacant leadership and any other important positions. For any organization to thrive, it must have solid bench strength. For you, as an owner or leader of an organization, you must possess solid bench strength so you can eventually take that leap from manager to owner to entrepreneur.

So how do you create this bench strength?

First, you must always transfer the knowledge and experience from the top. This aids in the education and development of future leaders. Any successful sporting organization is typically led by a great coach who is a great communicator and motivator. Coaches not only have the ability to build people up, they do this all while holding them to a high standard of accountability and ownership.

To build great bench strength you must build solid relationships across the generations.

These filtered down skills, talents, and values of this diverse group will strengthen the overall leadership.

Develop succession plans. Don't wait until the need for a leader is obvious! Identify and nurture high-potential members of the team. This group can be the first to leave if they are not properly recognized and developed.

Provide cross-departmental learning and exposure. This will develop a much better understanding of the overall organizational systems. This will also change the attitudes of your employees by offering them cross-training and making them more substantive and involved in your business. It greatly helps boost morale.

Offer executive coaching. Having an outsider's perspective who specializes in this process can be very beneficial to upcoming leaders in succession planning. This will also provide a mastermind-type, strategic-thinking process that will be very helpful early in the young talents' career paths.

Consistently assess this talent and provide mentoring support for new managers and divisional leaders. This will help to acclimate them to their new roles. Constantly give your new leaders insights to help them increase their effectiveness.

Always keep an open dialogue. What leadership skills are crucial to the company's success? What is the most important philosophy about your company's culture of leadership? What type of individual fulfills this culture of leadership? How are they willing to step up to fulfill this culture?

One final ingredient in succession planning will likely be influenced by work/life concerns. Organizations will need to find ways to help high-potentials balance their work and personal life responsibilities. Organizations must understand the impact that generational influences have on employees' views on career development.

Be sure to recognize, develop, support, and train your organization's young talent, and with the proper bench strength, you will surely have your winning team.

It all begins with having the proper attitude and implementing the process creating a strong bench. With a great Attitude comes great Actions and even greater Results!

CHAPTER 2:

BUDGET/ BEHAVIOR/ BELIEF

"Our only limitations are those we set up in our own minds."

Napoleon Hill, American Author

"B" represents Budget, Behavior, and Belief. For any business to be successful for the long term it must have and stick to a budget while the behavior of both the owner and the team of a business will determine how successful they become.

The budget is a crucial tool for the owner to understand one's numbers, expenses, cash flow, and how every line item in the business relates to the overall revenues. With a proper budget, you can track marketing expenses and how it impacts your revenues on a month-to-month basis. With a budget, you can track your payroll expense percentages as it relates to revenues last year, last month. The budget is the lifeblood and pulse of the business. For a business to be successful and long-lasting, the owner must always have his finger on that pulse.

The behavior of the business is also very important and this is shaped by both the owner and the team. Your behavior dictates your decisions which dictate your actions which dictate your results, and the bottom line in business is all about results!

The behavior is what everyone sees on the surface. However, it is what's below the surface that shapes this behavior. What you find first below the surface are your skills. You can increase your skills in any part of your business, and this goes for both the owner and the team. You can read books, take a course, attend workshops, and mentor other professionals to increase your skills. As you increase your skills you will possess the ability to make better decisions which will lead to more intentional actions which should increase your results.

Another part of your behavior is how you respond to your environment. Be very conscious of the environment of your workplace, your staff, your culture, and most importantly, the people you associate with. Look at the cleanliness of the car you drive and your office you keep. These are all everyday elements of the surroundings that will shape your environment and travel with you towards your success.

On the surface lies the behavior. Below the surface lies skills followed by belief – practicing how you believe your company to be. If you want to be the best in the industry, have the best team, provide the best service, you first have to believe that you are the best and can deliver in those areas. You can possess all of the skills in the world; however, if you don't believe in yourself and your team, all those skills are worthless.

What many people don't realize is their language is a crucial element of their identity and to their overall success. Your identity is very important. It encompasses your skills, beliefs, and values. With identity, you have to pay close attention to your *I Am's*. Your *I Am's* are so important because whatever word or words come after *I Am,* they are responsible for shaping your destiny. That is exactly how your belief system begins and thus your identity. For example, if you say "I am a great leader" and believe it, you'll be a great leader. If you say "I am passionate and energetic," then you will be passionate and energetic. If one of your team says "I am charging forward and conquering this project," then they will do just that – charge forward and conquer. One of my *I Am's* is "I am the Master of Knock It Out of the Park Leadership" which is where the title of this book came from.

The moment you believe in the language of your *I Am's* – kind of the old adage of practicing what you preach – is the moment you will develop your identity because it will require the use of your skills coupled with your values and believing exactly what you set out to do.

Be conscious of your behavior and all its invisible ingredients while keeping a good eye on your budget. Continue to practice and follow your beliefs and this will be one of those winning combinations that will help you and your business thrive.

CHAPTER 3:

COMMUNICATION AND CULTURE

"The most important thing in communication is to hear what isn't being said."

Peter Drucker, American-Austrian Consultant

Communication (or lack thereof) is the link between a successful or unsuccessful marriage, organization, team, or endeavor. Any time there is a breakdown in an organization, partnership, or endeavor it usually comes from a lack of communication. If you are married, you will know exactly what I'm talking about.

I'd like to discuss a man who I believe was a master of communication. He was great in his time and consistently made people stop and listen. Not just because he was a great man, but because he was a great communicator. This man was Dr. Martin Luther King, Jr.

I will share seven points of what you can practice and eventually master the art of communication, much the same way Dr. King did.

Passion – We all remember Dr. King as a very passionate speaker. That passion allowed his audience to feed off his energy and believe every word he spoke. When you bring passion and energy into your communication, you draw people in and make it almost impossible for them to tune out. What type of passion are you bringing with you when you speak?

Language – Dr. King only spoke of the possibilities. He used positive language to point out the benefits of taking the high road and how we can make a difference. By using positive language, he consistently made his message absolutely clear. Are you using positive uplifting language in your conversations and meetings with your team and/ or family?

Context − Dr. King was a master of establishing the historical context in his messages. He brought those historical stories into his speech and empowered people in his movement and sense of mission. What context do you share with your team to empower them to follow your movement or mission? People will always remember a story that captures their attention and emotion.

Authenticity − Dr. King always spoke from his heart. He clearly exemplified the example of leadership by consistently communicating his story. A story that embodied his life. His audience clearly understood that he was living his story.

I'll share that on several occasions during a coaching session with a client, he or she would share a challenge they were experiencing with a particular individual in their organization. They would go on and fill me in on the entire story of both sides. I simply always replied with the same question: "Have you had this conversation with them?" I also suggested to first ask the person, "Do I have your permission to speak from the heart in our conversation?" Authenticity in a conversation is the best element to deliver trust and cooperation from others.

Are you being truly authentic with your communication with others? In fact, what's your story? Can your team and clients clearly see that you are living your story? I believe that people buy you first, then your service or product second. Simply put, authenticity sells!

Practice – One of the most iconic speeches in history, the "I Have a Dream" speech, was a speech that was mostly spoken on the spot without any notes. What his audience didn't understand is that he had been working on that content for months and years prior during his other speaking engagements. He became very comfortable with his content as he experimented with what worked and didn't work.

I have had a YouTube channel for several years for which I produce weekly Monday morning videos: https://www.youtube.com/channel/UCfcjLSbh3G__vngFyE3qjvQ

I've spoken at many associations or events. Many have commented on how smooth my speaking presentations and videos are. That's only because they weren't witnesses to my practice time or my video blooper reels. My question to you is: How much do you prepare before you speak in front of your audience and team?

Vision – Dr. King's simple yet memorable phrase "I Have a Dream" lives on forever. Why? Because he used it consistently. He created a vision for all others to believe in and follow. What is your vision and have you clearly articulated that to your team of followers?

Connection – Dr. King mastered the ability to connect with his audience. This connection came from a place where he believed that together we can make a difference. It's an energy that you just can't fake. It's a connection that moves people to action. A connection is the purest form of communication. When you speak, are you making that type of connection by truly being present in your communication?

Practice and master these seven traits as part of your communication and you will be amazed how everyone else around you will begin to step up and show up more in business and in life. You'll also be amazed by what type of leader you become in the process.

NOW ON TO CULTURE...

"It's stunning to me what type of impact even one person can have if they have the right passion, perspective and are able to align the interest of a great team."

Steve Case, Author

In any business, it's always the internal culture that sets itself apart from the competition. A company's culture is the ingredients that will determine the type of employees and customers it attracts. Think of the culture Apple Inc. created that triggered diehard customers to camp out just to be the first to get their hands on a new phone or tablet.

Culture is the company's guide regarding all those unwritten yet important social issues that help give a business its character. It's that guide that lets every team member know what is acceptable and what is not. It is a collection of values that lets every team member know what is most important in terms of thoughts and behaviors.

When you really think of it, a company is a culture. It represents a group of people who share the same values and beliefs of the organization and why they do what they do. When you are clear on your culture, it creates the *why* of your company. When people are clear on their *why*, they will see the opportunity of their own ability within the organization thriving in the culture that is staying true to its purpose. Having a clear culture saves a company a whole lot of time in finding the right people who will fit in well with the rest of the team.

I have a client whose major challenge when we first started working together was employee attrition. He unfortunately burned through quite a few people over a two-year period. This was causing the company lots of extra time in training, stress, money, energy, not to mention slow revenue growth as they were constantly on the hiring and training cycle.

The first project we implemented was in the creation of a vision, mission, and culture for the organization. We had his team get involved with the process of creating it. A great process as when your team helps create it, they now own it. The end result was now that all is complete, the owner just seems to keep finding the right people that fit into the culture of the organization.

When an organization's culture is established, it essentially creates a group of people who come together around a common set of values and beliefs, as I spoke of in the last chapter. When sharing your values and beliefs, these form a sense of trust with others. Gaining the trust of others in an organization breeds confidence and advancement in the team and company. Trust also creates loyal raving fan customers just like in the case of Apple.

If you want to create the type of organization that people want to represent either as a team member or a raving fan customer, it is beneficial to first create that culture – where everyone will naturally thrive because their values and beliefs align with the values and beliefs of that particular culture of the organization.

It's not the products or services that bind a company together. It's not the size or the industry the company represents. It's the culture that drives everyone to do their best and give their best. From the owner down to the receptionist – they all share in this culture. The goal is not to hire people that simply have the skill set that your company needs. The goal is to hire people that believe in what you believe in and that is the culture of the organization.

CHAPTER 4:

MASTERY OF THE DELIVERY PROCESS

"Excellence is to do a common thing in an uncommon way."

Booker T Washington, American Educator

Delivery Mastery is about getting your products and services into your customers' hands when they want it the way they want it. Delivery Mastery is all about delivering what you said you would deliver when you said you would deliver it the way you said you would deliver it; anything less is unacceptable. Simply put, Delivery Mastery is essentially about making sure you consistently deliver on your promise!

There are four important areas of Delivery Mastery.

Supply Mastery

Be certain that you have the proper systems to measure the amount of stock in inventory to ensure consistent delivery of your products and services. There's nothing more frustrating to a customer than not being able to get what they want when they want it. Have you ever gone to a restaurant and ordered the special of the day only to have them tell you that they ran out – really? What impression did you have of that restaurant? Would you go back again? Chances are not likely!

Quality Mastery

You must deliver on the quality of your product or service with systematic consistency. McDonald's may not have the best food in the world; however, you know exactly what you're going to get every time, no matter where you are in the world. Your customer has to be confident that they can count on your consistency every time.

Easy to Buy Mastery

Be sure you are able to take all sorts of payments – cash, checks, credit, and debit cards. Not being able to honor any of these sources of payments may be a reason for someone not to use your services. Be sure that your website is easy to navigate or your potential buyer may give up and go elsewhere. Simply, make it easy for your customers to get what they want, when they want it, the way they want it!

A simple example of Easy to Buy Mastery: I was consistently taking my dry cleaning to a cleaner close to my home and office. I liked everything about them, except for one thing. They only took cash or checks, no credit cards. Not a big deal, however, I never carry a checkbook and I may sometimes for whatever reason not have enough cash in my wallet. Soon another dry cleaner opened close to my home and office. They not only provide a better more systematized service, but they also take cash, checks, and credit cards. Because they mastered easy to buy, they now have my business. Unfortunately, the prior business most likely lost and will lose a certain percentage of their business, simply because they didn't take credit cards.

Service Mastery

Don't look at customer service as a transaction; look at customer service as an interaction! Service Mastery is just the feeling your customers get from you and/or your team's interaction and service! Remember that customer service is not a department – customer service is an attitude.

When I think about Delivery Mastery, I think about Amazon Prime – you know exactly what you are going to get when you are going to get it. There is nothing better than clicking a button today and having it on your doorstep tomorrow. Make sure you fully understand that Delivery Mastery is the life blood of your business. Make it a priority to consistently deliver your absolute best to your customers. Give them what they want, when they want it, the way they want it. Consistently deliver on your promise, excel over your competition, and you'll be sure to create raving fans of your customers by excelling in Delivery Mastery!

CHAPTER 5:

EFFICIENCY EQUALS SUCCESS

"No matter how great the talent or efforts, some things just take time.

You can't produce a baby in one month by getting nine women pregnant."

Warren Buffett, CEO, Berkshire Hathaway

To remain on top in an increasingly competitive world, organizations must boost operational efficiency wherever possible. It's particularly important for small to medium-size businesses to operate efficiently, because they often have limited resources compared to larger organizations.

The following are a few tips to help your organization increase efficiency, reduce costs, improve customer satisfaction, and stay ahead of the competition.

- Culture: Great companies and organizations are great because they are very clear about their culture. Zappos serves as a great example as they have become almost as well known for their culture as they have for the shoes that it sells online.

  Zappos interviews and hires according to cultural fit first and foremost. It has established what the company culture is, and fitting into that culture is the most important thing managers look for when hiring. New employees are offered $2,000 to quit after the first week of training if they decide the job isn't for them. Ten core values are instilled in every team member. Employee raises come from workers who pass skills tests and exhibit increased capability, not from office politics. Portions of the budget are dedicated to employee team building and culture promotion.

  Great benefits coupled with a workplace that is fun and dedicated to making customers happy all fit in with the Zappos approach to company culture; when you get the company culture right, great customer service, and a great brand will happen on its own. This promotes a culture of happy employees, which ultimately leads to happy customers.

https://www.entrepreneur.com/article/249174

- Time Management: I can't say how many times I have heard "I just don't have enough time." Well, we all have the same amount of time. How we utilize that time is the difference in making things happen consistently. We need to get fully conscious of the value of our time. Measure where your time is being spent. Find where you can dump or delegate and identify the WIN (What's Important Now) formula to find what's going to present you with the highest ROI (Return on Investment) of your time.

  Time is money is not just a cliché, it's a fact.

- Create Effective Systems: Systems stand for *Saving Yourself Stress Time Energy and Money*. Many smaller businesses usually fail to implement systems under the false premise that they don't have the time to do so. However, how much is it costing the business by not having this system in place? A system is essentially an investment that consistently saves you time and money and continues to pay dividends as long as it's being utilized. The structure is what you need to run an effective organization and the systems are the backbone that creates that structure.

- Communication: Communication is the ingredient that will keep your organization running smoothly. However, the lack of communication is usually the downfall of many organizations. Effective communication between employees, partners, suppliers, and customers is a sure-fire way to keep your organization running efficiently.

  Are you running weekly team meetings? If yes, are they effective? Do you have a clear outline of how they are run? Are you having daily huddles with your team? Does your organization have a clearly defined and scheduled review process for all of your team?

  These are just a few questions and examples you can ask yourself in which to step up the process of increasing communication.

- Take Care of the Team: I cannot stress enough that your team is the glue that keeps your organization running effectively. Your job as a leader is to simply take care of your team. When you properly take care of your team, they will take care of your customer. Your customer will be happy, come back more often, spend more money, and tell their friends. This will deliver the organization the increase in revenues and profits which you want to see happening.

  Thirty+ years ago I wrapped up my 15-year ride in the restaurant business as a manager. A position I wouldn't recommend to anyone. I transferred from the original TGI Fridays in Fort Lauderdale, Florida to a brand new TGI Fridays in Aventura Mall in North Miami. I essentially transferred from a store that was totally synergetic to a totally opposite scenario. Through all the chaos as a new manager in a new store, I soon realized that the only true skill I really needed to apply on my shift was to make sure each and every member of the team was on their A-Game. From the waitresses, waiters, bartenders, barbacks, cooks, expediters, and dishwashers. Once I learned how to properly take care of the team, the team took care of the restaurant.

We all know the difference between exceptional, OK, and bad service. Exceptional service becomes an experience of where you're consistently being up-sold and you just go along for the ride. The food is delivered timely, fresh, and hot. The restaurant is clean and the service is exceptional. This only happens when the team is at their best, which only happens when the team is properly taken care of.

This brand-new chaos-filled Aventura, North Miami Fridays that I managed soon became the store of the division for two consecutive quarters in addition to having one of the top-performing front bars in the entire nation. This can only be achieved by having an exceptional team. The lesson is: take care of the team and they'll take care of you. It's that simple!

These are just a few tips on how to increase your company efficiencies to create more synergy, revenues, and profits. Put them in place, master them and you'll have an efficient running successful organization.

CHAPTER 6:

THE F-WORDS

"Friday is my second favorite F-word."

Anonymous

I'm going to tackle several F-words below that I believe are key to running successful organizations.

Fear – Fear is just the avoidance of having to do something unknown or unfamiliar. People simply avoid it because they haven't gone there before. Let's face it, we've all been there one time or another. The word fear can actually represent one of two meanings: *False Evidence Appears Real* or *Face Everything And Rise.* You have the choice of which one to apply. True growth starts at the end of our comfort zone and the only way to grow is to embrace our fears head-on.

Failure – Great teams and organizations fail fast, fairly often, and freely. When you embrace your fears, you move forward; sometimes you succeed, sometimes you fail. However, we all must get comfortable with failing forward to succeed.

I believe the most prominent example of failure without giving up is as follows:

Failed in business at age 21.

Was defeated in a legislative race at age 22.

Failed again in business at age 24.

Overcame the death of his sweetheart at age 26.

Had a nervous breakdown at age 27.

Lost a congressional race at age 34.

Lost a congressional race at age 36.

Lost a senatorial race at age 45.

Failed in an effort to become Vice President at age 47.

Lost a senatorial race at age 47.

Was elected President of the United States at age 52!

Based on this past record of failures, Abraham Lincoln had no right to think he could win the presidency of the United States. However, that didn't keep him from trying. Where would the advancement of our world actually be today if every time someone first failed in the past they chose not to try again? I'm sure Thomas Edison who failed 10,000 times before he succeeded and old Abe would have had an interesting answer to that question.

Fundamentals – Fundamentals are simply the systems and processes that you employ in your organization. It's all the important little things you do consistently to keep the team and organization moving forward synergistically. If you stop practicing the fundamentals that brought you success, you will soon find yourself stuck and wondering what happened to the wonderful momentum you were enjoying in your organization. You witness this in sports where a player stops doing all the little things he or she did to get them to where they are only to find themselves in a slump and wondering what happened. If you are not working hard to move forward and improve, you are simply moving backward.

Finance – For organizations to last, they must have financial stability. And to have financial stability, they must know their numbers inside and out. They must have the right metrics on a scoreboard they can read to make the proper shifts and decisions to keep the organization's cash flow running smoothly.

It's amazing that the number one reason most people go into business is to make money. Unfortunately, especially for many small business owners, it's usually the last thing they look at.

Focus – "The main thing is to keep the main thing the main thing." Focus on what moves the needle in your business forward the most. Not only for you as the leader. Everyone on your team must know their vital functions of what is most important in the success of your organization.

We are all dealt with distractions in our world on a daily basis. The year 2020 was a perfect example of how distractions could easily derail anyone. The world experienced a pandemic, business closings, the U.S. election with people fiercely opposing each other based on their political stance, demonstrations (I use this word loosely). A daily barrage of negativity from the media and all other sources of information as well as misinformation. If you were not extremely focused on where your time and energy were to be directed to produce results, you were swallowed up by the distracted world and it most likely cost you stress, time, energy, and money. All of which none of us can rightfully afford.

Friends and Associates — There was a great little book written by Ivan Misner and a couple of colleagues titled *Who's in Your Room?* It shares how the quality of your life depends on the quality of people in your life. How true — to be successful in both life and in business it all comes down to who you surround yourself with. If you're committed to becoming your absolute best, you need to associate with those who are committed to the same in their own life. Your success or failure is directly related to the company you keep. Case in point, be very conscious of who you let into your room.

Future — The future is what you make it, how you see it, and the work you do to make it real. When you're mastering these principles along with your entire organization, be clear on the path to accomplishing the company's mission and most important vital functions. You should have a bright future as you're pushing forward and onward.

Fun — We all have good days and bad days on the job. In the end, the only difference was whether you were having fun or not. When we are having fun in our professions, we simply achieve better results. Simply put, when you're having *fun* in business, you're in the *zone*, and when you're in the *zone* you're *cashing checks*. I hope in the end we're all in the business to cash checks.

Get clear on what F-words you need to incorporate into your organization and create an organization operating in the *zone* on which you are consistently cashing checks.

CHAPTER 7:

GOALS ARE S.M.A.R.T.

"People with goals succeed because they know where they are going."

Earl Nightingale, American Author

Goals are the pathway to reaching success. It is proven that all successful people are intensely goal-oriented. One of their rules of success is: It doesn't matter where you are coming from; all that matters is where you are going.

Goals are extremely important as they give you and your organization a sense of meaning and purpose – a sense of direction. Achieving your goals is what you think about most, what you want to get out of it, and how you are going to get it. Why? Because you become what you think about most of the time.

The size, scope, and detail of the goals you choose to think about most of the time is completely up to you. To unlock and unleash your full potential, shouldn't you then make it a habit of setting some high-achievement goals that will stretch you and your team to get the juices flowing in the accomplishing of it?

The reality is that the ultimate purpose of all human action is the achievement of personal happiness. Setting goals, working towards them day-by-day, and ultimately achieving them is the key to happiness in life.

Knowing all this, why would someone not set goals? Several reasons. They could fear the failure of not achieving them – failure hurts – so they sabotage themselves by not setting them or setting them way too low. They could think that they are not worthy enough to accomplish them. Actually, by not setting goals you are still creating your outcome, realize though that it just might not be the outcome that you truly desire.

How does one set good goals? First, you must make them S.M.A.R.T. goals. S.M.A.R.T. stands for *Specific, Measurable, Achievable, Results-Oriented,* and *Time-Frame Bound.* Let's take a look at these in greater clarity.

Specific: The greater clarity you have regarding your true goals, the more of your potential you will unleash. Invest whatever time is required to become absolutely clear on exactly what you want and how you can best achieve it. Where your focus goes, your energy flows. Because of this, it's absolutely essential to be specific about your goals.

Measurable: Make sure you can absolutely measure the results of your goal. An example would be setting an exact number of profits you want to achieve in your business as opposed to just more money.

Achievable: Make sure your goal is both a stretch that will make you go further than you have before, but also real enough that it will provide the proper belief in the attainment of that goal.

Results-Oriented: Be sure to have a visible clear outcome of what you want to obtain.

Time-Frame Bound: A goal is just a dream with a timeline attached so be extremely clear on when this goal is going to be accomplished.

A study done at Dominican University in California revealed that writing down your goals contributed to a 42% increase in goal achievement. What's more important is the study found adding an accountability partner works even better. Those who translated their goals into actions and committed to an accountability partner by providing weekly progress reports increased goal achievement by 78%.

Is a 78% increase in the probability of your success worth the effort? YOU BET IT IS!

Take a look at your goals and identify if they are S.M.A.R.T. goals. If they don't match up with what was just discussed, adjust your goals to get additional specificity.

CHAPTER 8:

HUMAN CAPITAL VALUE

"Treat employees like they make a difference, and they will."

James Goodnight, CEO of SAS Institute

What is your organization's understanding of human capital value? Human capital is defined as the collective skills, knowledge, experience, characteristics or other intangible assets of individuals that are viewed in terms of their value or cost to an organization.

The higher the individual human capital usually pays off with an increase in a worker's productivity. Higher worker's productivity usually pays off in a dripping down effect to increased margins of the organization.

One's human capital is created by how much that individual invests in their own education prior to joining the organization. That prior investment of education usually pays off in a higher pay grade to that individual.

A perfect example of a self-investment of human capital is as follows: I had the pleasure of meeting a gentleman that manages a hedge fund specializing in cryptocurrencies. He told me how he identified a trend, years back, and decided to invest 60 minutes a day in studying cryptocurrencies. He felt that 60 minutes a day in five years would make him an expert. He was right! Now he and the hedge fund that he manages are very successful in this area. His success is a direct result of his investment in his own human capital.

Having that type of education is the best investment in human capital as it will pay off in terms of higher productivity and results. This begs the question: What sort of education is your team consistently getting on their own and/or from the organization?

I have the extreme pleasure of coaching successful brothers/business partners that made two competitor acquisitions in a 10-month period. The most valuable asset of these acquisitions to their current organizational structure was not actually the database of business, nor was it the machinery and equipment, nor was it the additional revenues and earnings that came along.

As we aligned the different divisions into the overall organization, we ran behavioral assessments on all leadership personnel, and had team alignment days coupled with individual coaching sessions. We concluded that it was most definitely the human capital of leadership that came with the acquisitions. Now it's our job to simply leverage and continue to invest in these people to keep it that way.

We must be in understanding that our team is the number one most valuable asset in our organization (please refer to chapter 1 – All About Attitude). I hear all too often the customer comes first. My question is: Who takes care of your customers? Your team, of course.

Take better care of your team. Create an environment of accountability and ownership. Create an environment of consistent learning, praise, and advancement. Create the culture where your team is all-in and they, too, become raving fan marketers of the brand.

When you take care of your team, they will naturally take care of your customer, your customer will be happy, they will come back more often, tell their friends, and your organization will continue to grow.

The simple message here is your team matters most. Make an investment in their human capital, continue to expect the best from them and you'll be quite happy that you made your people your organization's number one priority.

DO YOU HAVE HAPPY CLIENTS OR RAVING FANS?

"Your customers are only satisfied because their expectations are so low and because no one else is doing better. Just having satisfied customers isn't good enough anymore.

If you really want a booming business, you have to create raving fans."

Ken Blanchard, American Author

In my days as a financial advisor, I learned a valuable lesson between 2000 and 2002. When the stock market was screaming along during the technology run and everyone thought they were the greatest stock pickers in the world, all was fine. When the dot-com bubble burst, all was not fine. The lesson that I learned up until that point was that I had a book of business of all accounts. When the adversity hit and really took hold, I distinguished the difference between accounts and clients. The accounts took no ownership, blamed me, pointed their finger, and left; my clients stayed. It was at that moment I realized if I am going to build a business, I want a practice of clients and not accounts.

The stakes of keeping your clients have gotten even higher with all the competition, pricing, online discounts, and instant gratification. We can't just have happy clients or satisfied customers anymore. We have to create more!

In business, you want to be unique and you want to build your brand. So how do you know that you are the brand that everyone automatically thinks of? How do you know if you are truly unique? Imagine a foursome playing golf – they are waiting to tee up on the 8th hole. During the wait, they start talking business and someone asks, "Do you know a good general contractor because my son needs some work done on his home?" If your name of your company does not roll off the tip of the other couple's tongue like lightning, you haven't built your brand and you are just not that unique yet.

Your job in business is not to be content with having satisfied or happy customers. Your job is not to just deliver the goods as they say. It is not to just live up to your customers' expectations. It is not to be confident that your happy customers will keep coming back again and again. Your job is to deliver absolutely "outside the box" awesome customer service. Your job is to create *raving fans* – those that act like disciples – who will go out and sing your praise to whomever they meet wherever they go.

So, how do we create raving fans? Let's stop and ask ourselves some questions first.

Are you sending your customers a small gift or a thank you after their first purchase? Have you branded yourself in a way that your clients will always remember you? Do you call and wish them Happy Birthday? Have you created the type of relationships with your customers in that they will want to go out and gather referrals for you? Have you created a customer experience that people talk about again and again? Do you simply say thank you for being a valued customer?

Take a moment and think back to a situation where you experienced the most amazing service possible. The type of experience that you just couldn't shut up about, I mean you absolutely had to tell everyone about it. What was it that made you feel that way? What did they do differently that was above and beyond? Lock this in because this is the beginning of where you create your own customer experience for them to feel the same way.

So, let's get into action. Go back and really take a look at your customer's experience. Create systems that will not only keep your customers coming back again and again, but empower them to be raving fan advocates that will sing your praise to whomever they meet wherever they go.

CHAPTER 9:

INVESTMENT IN YOURSELF

"Investing in yourself is the best investment you'll ever make. It will not only improve your life; it will improve the life of all those around you."

Robin Sharma, Canadian Writer

Warren Buffett is considered one of the greatest investors of all time and is consistently ranked among the wealthiest people in the world with a net worth north of $88 billion (October 2020). He is well known for his commitment to value investing, and when he makes recommendations, people listen. Someone had asked him what is his greatest investment of all time.

His answer was, "It's you. Invest as much as you can in yourself, you are your own biggest asset by far."

You simply will never get a better return than when you invest in yourself. Here are some ways to help you make the most of your investment.

Always stick with the important three: mind, body, spirit.

- Mind: Daily reading (could be as little as 15 minutes), journal, positive forward-thinking time. Our mind really is our most important asset. Unfortunately, many don't manage it properly.

- Body: Be sure to exercise, eat good food, drink plenty of water, get a good night's sleep. We only have one body to take us through life, be sure to take care of it.

- Spirit: Be grateful, pray, go to church, or just find some quiet time to connect with yourself. In this fast-paced world, many simply do not take the time for themselves to just be in a silent and calm state.

Create a morning Hour of Power daily routine.

Set aside that first hour in the morning to get grounded and create your day. Read, stretch, exercise, meditate, recite your affirmations, write in your gratitude journal, or the combination of. Your first hour of the day should be scheduled strictly for you.

Never stop learning.

One of the greatest secrets to Warren Buffett's success is that he is continuously learning. Learning doesn't end just because you're finished with school. The world is rapidly changing and we must not only stay up with it, but to be ultimately successful in business we need to actually stay ahead of it.

- Consistently read.

- Attend conferences, seminars, and masterminds.

- Take an online course.

- Talk to people and ask them questions (listen more than you talk).

- Research something you are interested in.

- Hire a coach.

Surround yourself with excellence.

"It's better to hang out with people better than you. Pick out associates whose behavior is better than yours and you'll drift in that direction." – Warren Buffett

Spend time getting to know yourself.

Your time is extremely valuable and precious. Spend some of it getting to know yourself better.

These practices can help you find out who you truly are:

- Meditate (even if you think you can't meditate).

- Do yoga.

- Write morning pages or journal.

- Find hobbies that you enjoy (and actually do them).

Business can sometimes be a hectic journey. Obstacles will pop up when you least expect them. As leaders we always have lots to manage: you have your team, customers, purveyors, partners, shareholders, you have payroll, deadlines, expectations, and plenty more to think about. Many times, a business owner or leader will take care of all of the above while leaving out one thing – themselves. They don't schedule a time for them. It was taught to me when I first became a coach to "take care of your number one client first." That number one client is you!

Invest as much as you can in yourself starting right now, and you will see returns beyond anything you could dream of. Remember along the way that success in life is not about the destination but about the journey. Invest in yourself, enjoy the journey and you just may positively impact some people along the way.

CHAPTER 10:

JUDGMENT AND ASSESSMENTS IN HIRING

"Good judgment is the result of experience and experience is the result of bad judgment."

Mark Twain, American Writer

I find it interesting that throughout my career I've heard business owners, leaders, and managers say, "I read their résumé, went with my gut instinct, and hired them on the spot." Not quite a judgment call in the hiring process that I would recommend.

The definition of Judgment is *the ability to make considered decisions or come to sensible conclusions.* It's sensible conclusions we're looking to execute in the hiring process.

Yes, as leaders, we sometimes have to make judgment calls, quick decisions, based on the information we have. However, when it comes to hiring and building a team, I truly believe in the old rule of "hire slow – fire fast."

We covered earlier the importance of creating a culture to attract the right people to fit into our organization. At the same time, we also have to get the right people in the right seats. Going with your gut instinct doesn't always properly execute on that rule.

In business and building solid organizational strength there is always a process. In hiring, I would never recommend leaving it to guesswork or a gut instinct. There is an extensive process and part of that process is to use assessments to get a proper read on people's behavioral patterns.

There are many types of behavioral/personality type assessments – Myers-Briggs, Wonderlic, as well as others; however, I use DISC both in my own hiring and coaching process as well as for all my clients.

The DISC is composed of four different personality traits/behaviors which are Dominance (D), Influence (I), Steadiness (S), and Conscientiousness (C).

- D personalities tend to be more confident and are mostly focused on bottom-line results.

- I personalities are more open and place their emphasis on building relationships as well as influencing others.

- S personalities are usually dependable, they like a steady pace, and place an emphasis on cooperation and sincerity.

- C personalities are all about accuracy, quality, and competency.

Most of us are usually inherent in two of the four behaviors. Certain behaviors simply fit better in different parts of the organization. You wouldn't want a free-spirited type salesperson behind a desk running spreadsheets eight hours a day. Nor would you want someone who is reserved that shies away from rejection cold calling throughout the day. It simply doesn't work.

These above behaviors also act as a double-edged sword. Part of your behavior serves you, and part of it doesn't. By utilizing the DISC personal assessment process in your organization, it will deepen your understanding of yourself as well as others. This will create a newfound clarity of your own personal behaviors to understand

and know when to shift to better serve yourself as well as others.

DISC profiling levels the playing field by providing leaders the proper information for communicating and coaching their team more effectively. Leaders become more naturally effective when they understand the disposition and preferred working styles of their employees and team members.

Utilizing DISC personal assessments in your organization raises self-awareness – constructive change begins with self-knowledge. DISC profiling shows you how to respond to conflict, what motivates or stresses you out, and how to solve problems.

The DISC model simply provides a common language people can use to better understand themselves and those they interact with; the use of this knowledge reduces conflict while improving working relationships. Using the DISC system effectively in your organization will improve teamwork, communication, and productivity in the workplace which are all active ingredients in building solid organizational strength.

CHAPTER 11:

KPI'S ARE THE FUEL TO YOUR ORGANIZATION'S ENGINE

"When performance is measured, performance improves. When performance is measured and reported, the rate of improvement accelerates."

Thomas T. Monson, American Religious Leader and Author

Herein lies the question: Are KPI's the oil to your engine, the fuel to your organization, the key components that move the speedometer forward in your sales and revenues?

KPI's (**Key Performance Indicators**) are the measurable values that demonstrate how effectively a company is achieving its key business objectives and goals. Organizations use KPI's at multiple levels to evaluate their success at reaching targets. High-level KPI's may focus on the overall performance of the organization, while low-level KPI's may focus on processes such as sales, marketing, or number of calls.

Whatever Key Performance Indicators are selected, they must reflect the organization's goals, they must be a key to its success, and they must be quantifiable.

Key Performance Indicators should also be S.M.A.R.T. – Specific, Measurable, Attainable, Results-Oriented, and Time-Bound.

Ask yourself these questions below when putting together your company's KPI's:

- Is your objective **Specific**?

- Can you **Measure** progress towards that goal?

- Is the goal realistically **Attainable**?

- How **Relevant** is the goal to your organization?

- What is the **Time-frame** for achieving this goal?

Once you have your S.M.A.R.T. Key Performance Indicators in place, they should be consistently evaluated and re-evaluated based on the progress of the organization.

Key Performance Indicators can be a great measuring tool when linked to considering promotions, bonuses, and salary/wage increases.

- To be truly effective you should be measuring Key Performance Indicators in all areas of the organization – in fact, for each position.

- You can measure a Key Performance Indicator in the percentage of its income that comes from return customers.

- In sales you might measure the performance by the numbers of people the salesperson both calls and sells to each day.

- You may measure how effective your marketing campaigns are at generating new clients, conversion, and sales.

- You can measure your organization's financial health by analyzing readily available working capital that could be used to meet any short-term obligations.

- You can measure the percentage of customer calls answered within the first three rings as a KPI.

- Understand that a company cannot manage what it is not properly measuring. What is also important to remember is in what you test and measure, you usually increase.

What makes a KPI effective?

A Key Performance Indicator is only as valuable as the action it inspires. A KPI must always effect a positive change. Understand that when team members have something positive to strive for it adds an element of competition into their daily routines. When they aim for and achieve their own personal goals, this will not only have a positive effect on the running of the business as it will have a positive effect on the team as well.

In terms of developing a strategy for formulating KPI's, your team should start with the basics and understand what your organizational objectives are, how you plan on achieving them, and who can act on this information. This should be an iterative process that involves consistent feedback.

Once you establish your KPI's, position them by communicating them well and enrolling your team in the process and outcome. Understand that the truth is that KPI's are only as valuable as you make them. KPI's require time, effort, and employee buy-in to live up to their high expectations. However, their true potential value remains in the hands of those that use them and use them well.

CHAPTER 12:

THE POWER OF LEVERAGE

"Compound interest is the eighth wonder of the world.

He who understands it, earns it; he who doesn't, pays it."

Albert Einstein, Theoretical Physicist

What is the application of leverage in an organization? Leverage is simply about getting more with less. More productivity, more results, more money with less effort, less energy and investment.

The actual definition of Leverage is as follows:

Leverage is the ability to influence a system, or an environment, in a way that multiplies the outcome of one's efforts without a corresponding increase in the consumption of resources.

In other words, leverage is the advantageous condition of having a relatively small amount of cost yield a relatively high level of returns.

To apply the Power of Leverage into any organization you must first commit to the implementation of Systems. System stands for *Saving Yourself Stress Time Energy* and *Money*. Leverage is simply all about systemizing the routine. In other words, a business system is a repeatable process that produces a profit. Think of systems as the grease in the business that gives it the ability to run smoothly.

The first place to start leveraging your organization is with your people. Leverage is first in getting more from yourself, enhancing your own business knowledge and skills, developing yourself personally and professionally in addition to increasing your stamina and energy. Leverage next starts with replacing yourself or much of what you do personally. Leverage is in enrolling, empowering, and properly managing your team. Leverage is all about proper time management, skill management, and proper training. All this will gain you the ability to get more from your team by properly training them, treating them well, and giving them space to express their true talents.

Once you are leveraging your business by having systems in place you will continually get a return on the investment of your initial time and planning. The time it took you to administer the systems and train your people will hit a breakeven at some point and then will continue to pay you dividends for many years to come.

CAUTION – For smaller business owners, don't use the lack of time as an excuse for not implementing the proper systems. Ask yourself: How much *Stress, Time, Energy,* and *Money* has it cost me already by not having this system in place? This question should usually get you to slow down long enough to realize the value of implementing it now.

Several areas of Leverage to consider for your business:

- People Leverage: Utilizing your people's talents, skills, contacts, credibility, and resources. You can also leverage certain talent within your team to train your team.

- Technology Leverage: Fully utilizing the latest technology to increase your speed and efficiency. You can also leverage outside sources like Upwork or Fiverr to create anything while you sleep for a very low cost. The leverage of online meetings using Zoom took off with the 2020 pandemic. Owning that particular stock early was also another type of leverage.

- Time Leverage: Managing your time more effectively is extremely important. Making sure your team is managing their time effectively by truly understanding their vital functions within the organization. Improper leveraging of time can be a killer in productivity and margins in an organization.

- Assessment Leverage: Using behavioral assessments to position the right people in the right places, with the right plan (refer to chapter 10).

- System Leverage: Will move the business away from people dependency to system dependency. This will create the organization that you can one day sell (if that is eventually your plan).

Be committed to applying the power of leverage in all areas of your organization and you will continue to reap the benefits of getting more with less.

CHAPTER 13:

MENTORS ARE MOLDERS

"One could have no smaller or greater mastery than the mastery of oneself."

Leonardo da Vinci, Italian Polymath

Who are your mentors and are you applying what you've learned from them to mold yourself to be a great mentor yourself?

The actual definition of a Mentor is as follows:

An experienced and trusted adviser, an experienced and trusted person who gives another person advice and help, especially related to work or school, over a period of time; someone who teaches or gives help and advice to a less experienced and often younger person.

Throughout our years, we've all had certain mentors in our life that have impacted us in the way we think and act, who molded our belief system as well as our habits. Certain mentors along your way most likely have actually been a pivotal point in your life that projected you in the direction of where you are today.

Brad Sugars, the Founder of ActionCOACH, mentioned not only was it him attending a conference and meeting the late, great Jim Rohn, but more importantly, the conversations that he had with Jim Rohn that led his life in a certain direction.

Personally, I've had the privilege of meeting a few late greats such as Zig Ziglar, Dr. Robert Schuler, Christopher Reeve AKA Superman, Og Mandino, and others. I've had the honor to meet Colin Powell, General Norman Schwarzkopf, Pat Riley, Lou Holtz, President Bush, Tony Robbins, and many others. I have documented notes of their character traits as well as notable impactful quotes they shared, all of which some way or another have impacted me in a compounding type way.

Some of my mentors have come from the great books I've read along the way like *Think and Grow Rich* by Napoleon Hill, *The Psychology of Winning* by Dennis Waitley, *How to Win Friends & Influence People* by Dale Carnegie, *Dare to Win* by Mark Victor Hansen, and *Unlimited Power* by Tony Robbins, just to name a few. Biographies on General George Patton, George Washington, Ben Franklin, Abraham Lincoln, and others have also had a profound impact on me.

I share this with the understanding that we all inherit certain qualities from all of the people we meet throughout our lives. Whether we just heard them speak, read their book, met them at an event, or were graced by their presence personally.

Some of our first mentors were our parents who instilled certain qualities and values in us that we live by today. It could have been a teacher in school that took the time to listen and guide us. It could be a leader of an organization you represented that has profoundly impacted you in a positive and productive way. It could have just simply been someone that witnessed more in you than you witnessed in yourself that created the possibilities for you to go for it with more confidence than you had before.

South Florida was home to a couple of extraordinary mentors. One was Wayne Huizenga, who died on March 22, 2018, in his home in Fort Lauderdale. Wayne Huizenga brought us Waste Management, Blockbuster Video, Auto Nation, the Florida Marlins and Florida Panthers. He was also an owner of the Miami Dolphins for 15 years. In 1999, he and his wife Marti donated $4 million to Nova Southeastern University that led to the Huizenga School of Business and Entrepreneurship.

The Huizenga family has donated countless millions to many charities like the American Heart Association, the American Cancer Society, the Make a Wish Foundation, Kids in Distress, and many other great causes.

Many that served under or alongside Wayne say, "The entrepreneurial mindset, the pep talks, and the time he took to provide insight and guidance were absolutely invaluable."

Another was Jim Moran AKA "The Courtesy Man." Jim was an automotive pioneer who made a significant impact here in South Florida. His career spanned more than six decades, before his passing on April 24, 2007. His lifetime achievements were recognized by his 1996 Horatio Alger Association of Distinguished Americans Award and his 2005 induction into the Automotive Hall of Fame, the single greatest honor in the international motor vehicle industry.

In 1984, Moran founded the Youth Automotive Training Center (YATC), located in Deerfield Beach, Florida as a privately funded program that offers basic automotive repair training, GED and academic preparation, and life skills proficiency for at-risk young people.

In 2000, he established The Jim Moran Foundation with the mission to improve the quality of life for the youth and families of Florida through the support of innovative programs and opportunities that meet the ever-changing needs of the community.

The Morans donated $1 million to fund a cardiovascular intensive care unit at Holy Cross Hospital in Fort Lauderdale. The Morans and JM Family Enterprises gave a combined $6 million in 2000 to build the Jim Moran Heart and Vascular Center and another five-year, $26 million donation for the Jim Moran Heart and Vascular Research Institute that began in 2006.

The Jim Moran Institute for Global Entrepreneurship was established in 1995 at Florida State University through a $1.8 million gift. The purpose of the entity was to provide a wide range of entrepreneurial services at no charge. In 2015, the Jim Moran Foundation donated another $100 million to Florida State University – the school's largest donation in history – to create what will be the nation's largest interdisciplinary, degree-granting school of entrepreneurship.

JM Family Enterprises which is headquartered in Deerfield Beach, Florida is recognized as one of Fortune's "100 Best Places to Work in America."

In Tallahassee, the state Rep. Jack Seiler, D-Wilton Manors, led the 120-member chamber in a moment of silence to honor Moran. "This individual was one of the most generous, and one of the most philanthropic persons," Seiler said. "He spent his whole life giving back to others."

Whether they be currently living, deceased, read about, met with, lived with, worked with or led by, we simply all have certain people who had a mentorship type impact on the quality of our lives. As leaders both in business and life, it is our responsibility to become our absolute best so we can pass these mentored values and qualities of greatness on to others. Master this quality as this is one of the core ingredients of building organizational strength.

CHAPTER 14:

UTILIZING THE WORD NO

"It's only by saying no that you can concentrate on the things that are really important."

Steve Jobs, Apple Co-Founder

What's the common denominator in the world's most successful people, people like Warren Buffett, Elon Musk, Richard Branson, Steve Jobs, Henry Ford, or even Thomas Edison?

When you think of Warren Buffett as one of the most successful investors in the world, Elon Musk for Space-X, PayPal or Tesla, Richard Branson for The Virgin Group of companies, Steve Jobs with Apple, Henry Ford for the Model T and the V-8 motor, or even Thomas Edison for his many inventions, you typically think of these highly successful individuals and of all the things they created or did.

What's also interesting about these successful people are you see them as a more relaxed and less stressed individual, and yet they accomplish or have accomplished so much more.

This begs the question: What's their secret?

The simple truth behind their notable accomplishments didn't necessarily come from the things they said yes to, rather the success lies in what they said NO to. These mega-moguls truly understand how valuable their time is, and with that they have no problem consistently saying NO to the things that don't serve their primary focus.

Warren Buffett once famously said, "The difference between successful people and really successful people is that really successful people say no to almost everything."

Do you have a problem saying no? Are there times when you say yes to things for the fear of disappointing someone else?

Have you ever said yes to something or someone that you really wanted to say no to? How did that make you feel afterward? Were you left feeling energized and focused or frustrated and stressed?

Early in my career as a coach, I had a client named Barbara. Like many new entrepreneurs, Barbara had a challenge saying no. She was letting other people's so-called emergencies become her emergency. She was donating her time to several different charities. Barbara was simply a pleaser of others. She actually felt guilty if she didn't make others happy. All this was sucking up her time and causing frustration.

After some probing questions, and finally realizing that this strategy obviously wasn't working for her, she got a grip on being more intentional with her time. She dropped all the charitable foundations except for one which was closest to her heart. She became more aware of how valuable her time was. She got really clear on exactly who was an ideal client for her business. She positioned those clients more intentionally on the rules of the game up front. Most importantly, she simply learned how to say no to what didn't serve her business plan. I'm happy to share that Barbara now has a business that works for her, she works less, makes more money, and most importantly, spends more time with the ones she loves.

To be ultra-successful, you need to be very clear of your vital functions, the one or two things that truly move you towards your ultimate goal. You will find when you are laser-focused on what's most important, it becomes easy to say no to everything else. Only now with this intentionalism of purpose will the true priorities take precedence.

Understand that every time you say yes to something that is clearly important to your cause or purpose, you are saying no to something that is not. This in itself creates tremendous personal and professional freedom.

At the Apple Worldwide Developers Conference in 1997, Steve Jobs shared where his success came from and the importance of saying no. "People think focus means saying yes to the thing you've got to focus on. But that's not what it means at all. It means saying no to the hundred other ideas that are out there. You have to pick carefully. I'm actually as proud of the things we haven't done as the things I have. Innovation is saying no to 1,000 things." These are obviously the words of a highly focused individual.

If you were to ask me to partake in a particular task that is not in my most important column, I would be able to easily reply with a firm no. It actually sets some people back a bit with my rapid-fire response of no to a certain question or request. I just simply state that I have a precalculated yes and no column of what serves me, my organization, my purpose, and what doesn't. When you possess this type of clarity, it's easy to say no to what's not important to your cause.

Let me be clear that this isn't an interpretation to be selfish. We always must be open to "pay it forward" and give ourselves to others. However, be clear that it still serves our cause of what's important to us, on where we want to share our value, wisdom, time, experience, and money. For instance, there are thousands of different charitable foundations out there in this world. You can't possibly share your time and money with all of them. Like Barbara, pick the one or few that are closest to your heart and back them. It's this clarity that keeps you centered on what's most important in you giving back.

Remember, everyone is given the same amount of time. What makes a difference is what you choose to say yes to and what you choose to say no to in the value of your time. Create your yes and no column based on what serves you, your organization, and your purpose. When you finally create this clarity, you'll actually enjoy a new journey of living in the world of freedom in knowing what is truly important of your valuable time while saying no to everything else.

CHAPTER 15:

THE BIG O'S

"Responsibility equals accountability equals ownership. And a sense of ownership is the most powerful weapon a leader, team or organization can have."

Pay Summit, Basketball Coach

What's the Big O's in the creation of a successful organization? What's the Big O's that are either moving you and your organization forward or actually inhibiting your growth? The Big O's are most importantly and always: first Ownership, followed by Opportunity and/or the Opportunity cost associated with the decisions you either make or don't make.

First, let's tackle the word Ownership. The definition of the word Ownership is *the act, state, or right of possessing something, being an owner.* https://dictionary.cambridge.org/us/dictionary/english/ownership

The formal definition of what we'll be addressing is an *attitude of accepting responsibility for something and taking control of how it develops.* https://www.macmillandictionary.com/us/dictionary/american/ownership

Many of us want more. More out of life, more out of business, more out of our team, just more. However, what are the ingredients to produce more? What does it take to develop a more empowered and enrolled team, to become a better leader, a better business person, or to create a winning organization? What does it take to grow mentally or to grow physically?

What it takes is we have to become the person that takes the action to fulfill and accomplish all our dreams, goals, and plans. The only way we can do that is we simply have to take full 100% ownership and responsibility.

True growth starts at the end of our comfort zone. We must get comfortable being uncomfortable to grow. If you go to the gym to lift weights or take a class, how comfortable is it the first time you go? How comfortable do you feel the day after? Many of us will state, not very comfortable at all. When you lift weights, the only way to grow your muscles is to lift heavier weights. It's uncomfortable, however, it's what gives us the gains we're looking for. So many out there are ready to quit when it gets too hard. They find excuses for why they can't. They simply are not willing to embrace the uncomfortable, they are not willing to own it.

It's not any different if you are looking to grow your organization. You have to get comfortable with the uncomfortable. You have to develop yourself more before you take on the next step. You have to be willing to embrace the uncomfortable. You simply have to own it!

My belief is that great leadership is simply in the act of taking full ownership in oneself. Early in my career, I was working with a business owner who had a rather large challenge with employee retention. His practice actually had a turnover rate of 100%+ over a two-year period. As we sat down and started to talk, he shared his frustrations about how his team had no accountability or ownership within the organization.

I simply started to ask questions: "Do you have a Vision, Mission, and Culture statement in place? Do you have position agreements in place for all your staff? Do you follow a strict 90-day review process? Do you run weekly meetings?" The answer to all these questions was repeatedly, "No!" I went as far as to ask: "Do you even speak to them at all?" His answer was, "Not really as I'm afraid they're just going to ask me for more money." Wow, talk about a disconnect from the pulse of the organization and team.

We agreed to start working together. For his first piece of homework, I gave him a little exercise which was for him to write down all of the people that had left his organization in the prior two years and why they left. Interestingly enough, he came back the following week with his completed homework. When I asked to share what showed up for him, he proceeded to give me all the reasons why each one of those individuals that left possessed something that was wrong with them.

With that I encouraged him to partake in the same exercise again, but doing it a little bit differently this time. In addition to sharing why they left, I also instructed him to write down what he could have done better as an owner and leader and what he will or no longer do in the future to once and for all fix this challenge for good. When we spoke the following week, I asked if he had completed his work. With an exhausted "Yes," he exclaimed that it was a lot harder exercise this time. "Why?" I asked. "Because I had to look at myself instead of them." Hmm, harder simply because he had to own it. This exercise was designed for him to actually own this challenge and understand that it was actually him that created this dilemma.

Once he became aware and owned his inadequacies, we were able to get to work. We started the process by running behavioral assessments on him and the entire staff. We defined his organization chart to get clear on all the key players. With the help of the entire leadership team we created a vision, mission, and culture of the organization. We implemented weekly meetings to bring everyone into the fold and to increase communication. We implemented position agreements with defined roles, responsibilities, and expectations for each of the staff along with a strict 90-day review process.

After creating all the structure for accountability in his organization, his entire behavior shifted to that more of a leader. He spent more time out of his office with the team as opposed to the prior habit of hiding in his office with the door closed. His team stepped up as they were all along waiting for him to put the structure of accountability in place. His retention dramatically improved and the respect of his team grew as well.

This entire process increased accountability, ownership, and employee retention. It created the identification of his key players that would help run the business for him! Most importantly, this process grew him as a leader simply because he chose to own it! There are no bad teams, only bad leaders. When you own the organization and team's results whether good or bad, only then can you represent yourself as the true leader the organization expects you to be.

While having an entirely different conversation with another business owner, he proceeded in telling me how bad his company's prior year was and how everything he couldn't control was a contributing factor of why it was unsuccessful. He proceeded in sharing all the reasons why.

I just let him vent and get it all out. At the end of that conversation, I asked, "Well, what's your number for this year?" He asked, "What do you mean?" I replied, "What's the dollar figure that you want to generate in revenues this year in your business?" Surprisingly, he gave me a relatively low number, which caught me off guard. I ask him why such a low number? And again, he went into a rant about how everything that's going on outside of his business that he couldn't control will affect the future potential revenue stream of his business.

I then asked him another question, "What was the best year you ever had in your business revenue-wise?" He shared with me a very nice number. A number that was much more to my liking. I then asked, "Well, what did you do that year?" As success leaves clues, we should investigate past success to see what we did so we can replicate it, do it again, and have the same type of success. His reply stunned me as he shared, "Oh, that had nothing to do with me. All the stars aligned. I got lucky. There's no way that my practice could replicate that same result again." Really, you have a bad year because you couldn't control all the outside circumstances. You have a good year and it was because of all the outside circumstances that you once again didn't control.

The lesson in these stories is that in both good and bad, simply own your results. Just own it! When you, your team, or your organization does well, own it. Own it because you worked hard. You did the prep work, you did whatever it took to create it, you empowered your team to follow through, that success was created because you were in control. If you, your team, or organization doesn't do well, own it. Learn from it. Make the necessary adjustments. Control everything within the four walls of your business as opposed to focusing on what you can't control.

When we take 100% responsibility and ownership for everything we do and the results we receive, only then can we learn and grow. When we shift to blaming and using excuses, we simply defer all control of our destiny away. No longer are we in charge. We are leaders, it is our 100% responsibility to own everything that happens in our organizations as well as in our life. Most importantly, as a leader of an organization, when you own it only then will your team own it. As in chapter 1 on attitude, you're the catalyst, you're the magnet that lifts everyone else around you up.

Take control of your destiny, own it, and only then will the future be based on your plan as opposed to what's going on outside the four walls of your business. In addition, and only then when you own it will the second O of opportunities begin to present themselves.

"A pessimist sees the difficulty in every opportunity; an optimist sees the opportunity in every difficulty."

Winston Churchill, United Kingdom Former Prime Minister

For every opportunity, you take advantage of some form of return or a cost for those we delay or pass on. Opportunities present themselves every day; however, only when you are open and truly ready to receive it, apply it and take action on it will it deliver the rewards you are looking for.

There's a story of an African farmer who owned vast acres of land. He continued to hear stories of how many other farmers were becoming millionaires by discovering and mining diamonds across the continent. This farmer decided to sell his farm, take the proceeds, and venture on his quest to find and mine his own diamonds so that he could also become rich in millions. He searched far and wide, long and hard, only to never discover the precious diamonds he was looking for. Finally, old, tired, and rejected, he threw himself in a river and drowned.

Meanwhile, the farmer who bought his farm happened to come across a small stream while walking the land one day and noticed a big shiny stone in the stream. Amazed by its beauty, he decided to bring it home and place it on the mantel over his fireplace so he could continually admire his amazing find.

Several weeks later a man was visiting him and approached the large stone on the mantel, took it in his hand to feel the weight and admire it, and almost fainted as he realized what it was. The farmer noticing his faintness asked if he was all right. The man replied, "Yes, of course, I'm OK, however, do you have any idea what this big stone is?" The farmer replied that it simply was a beautiful stone that he found in a nearby stream that he placed in his home to admire. The visitor then shared that the stone was actually the largest diamond ever mined from the African continent. The farmer really couldn't believe it as he shared that there were many other stones just like it in the stream. They now discovered and confirmed that this was the largest diamond mine on the entire continent.

The prior farmer had actually unknowingly owned free and clear the largest diamond mine on the entire continent of Africa. However, not knowing this, he followed through on his desire and went searching all over the continent for diamonds that were right underneath his very own feet all along.

The lesson of this story is that opportunities present themselves every day, but only when you are clear on exactly what you are looking for. When you have truly given yourself permission to receive it only then will you recognize it. Second, sometimes instead of going elsewhere to look for what you want or what you think you may need, you may want to first look in your own organization as you may just be standing on the diamond mine that you've all along been searching for.

In the previous chapter, I mentioned the common denominator in the world's most successful people like Warren Buffett, Elon Musk, Richard Branson, Steve Jobs, Henry Ford, and Thomas Edison who all knew what to say no to.

As you become more conscious of taking advantage of opportunities, you first must be clear on exactly what opportunities to act on and what ones to pass on. You can't get caught chasing shiny objects. Only when you are clear on your vital functions and what's most important in moving your organization forward will you be able to make the right choices.

Opportunity cost is simply about addressing these choices. Examples could be the opportunity cost of making a large investment in buying and folding a competitor's company into your organization to capture a larger market share, or passing on that decision that ends up with you consistently battling them or whoever else acquired them for that market share. You also have to weigh in the extra expenses and team you're taking on as well as integrating them into your organization's culture.

How awesome would it be if you actually knew the outcomes of these decisions in advance? Unfortunately, no one ever has that privilege. In these cases, a choice between the two options still must be made.

In both business and life, you must consistently weigh your options and potential outcomes in these decisions. Let's explore a few examples. What's the Opportunity cost of letting your ego get in the way of your decision-making process or procrastinating on decisions too long? What's the Opportunity cost of staying inside your comfort zone and not reaching for what's possible? What's the Opportunity cost of not investing in yourself or your team? What's the Opportunity cost of not having an accountability partner or a coach to help you identify your blind spots or having someone to ask the tough questions that no one else is willing to ask? What's simply the Opportunity cost of not taking action on something when you know it's the right thing to do? These are the questions you should be asking yourself.

In business it all comes down to the bottom line. Get clear on your intention, identify what opportunities serve that intention, give them your immediate attention, confer with your mastermind group, take action, don't procrastinate, test and measure the ROI on that action, and most importantly, take full ownership. And only then will you be well on your way to taking advantage of the big O's.

CHAPTER 16:

PERSEVERE TO PROFITS

*"Perseverance is not a long race;
it is many short races one after another."*

Walter Elliot, British Politician

Small businesses continue to play a vital role in the economy of the United States by producing almost 50% of the private non-farm GDP. In 2014, according to U.S. Census Bureau data, statistics show that about 40% of small businesses fail in their first year, 50% fail by their fifth year, and only about 20% of businesses will survive their 10th year in business. Pretty alarming stats.

What are the reasons why so many businesses fail? Could it be a lack of capital or financing? Could it be that the business owner surrounded themselves with the wrong people or chose the wrong partner? Could it be that they didn't install and apply the right systems or structure in the business? Or could it be that they simply burned out?

Michael Gerber wrote a great book called *The E-Myth Revisited*. In the book, he describes the Technician, the Manager, and the Entrepreneur. Most smaller business owners are great technicians. However, to succeed they must graduate on to manager then on to entrepreneur to ultimately be successful in business and in life.

Another reason why people fail is they lack the perseverance and stamina to get through all they need to get through to succeed. To *persevere to profits* we must keep on keeping on. Businesses sometimes get fixated on their top-line number, how much revenue they are generating. I say who cares, *persevering to profits* is all about the bottom line, it's all about what you put in the bank, what you put in your pocket, not necessarily what you put on the scoreboard.

Early in my career, I acquired a referred client named Jim who was instructed to read Michael Gerber's *E-Myth* before calling me. Jim had been in business for 35 years and had simply lost his passion for the business. During our initial conversation, I had asked about his revenue and profit history in particular the prior year. His answer was, "I'll have to check with my accountant." This was May of the following year and he was uneducated on exactly what was produced the prior year or any other year at that. He mentioned that they have done well and he was essentially happy with that. Jim, unfortunately, like many smaller business owners I learned early in my career, simply didn't know his numbers. Lesson number 1, if you don't know your numbers inside and out, you can't *persevere to profits*.

The first exercise for Jim was to create a budget, taking his prior year numbers both top and bottom line, adding 15% growth and budgeting out the entire year. An exercise that he was not quite excited about at first as he has only avoided it for the prior 35 years in business. With the budget completed, I had Jim import his actual monthly numbers as they came in and compared them to his budgeted numbers.

At first, he didn't readily have any answers to my questions pertaining to certain line expense items. However, he would do his investigation and have the answer the following week. This process, as tedious as it was for him, transferred Jim within four months to knowing his numbers inside out. Years 36 and 37 which we worked together were his two best years ever in the business prior to selling the business and retiring. Jim took ownership, did the work, and eventually *persevered to profits*.

For you to *persevere to profits*, do you actually have what it takes to persevere through cash flow challenges? Do you have what it takes to persevere in creating the internal culture to attract the right people to create your dream team? Do you have what it takes to persevere in applying the right systems and solutions to run your business synergistically? Do you have what it takes to simply persevere when everything seems to be going against you?

The meaning of Perseverance: *steadfastness in doing something despite difficulty or delay in achieving success.*

In the book *Think and Grow Rich* by Napoleon Hill, chapter 8 is "Decision – The Mastery of Procrastination." Procrastination is essentially on the opposite end of perseverance. In that chapter, there is a story of how we became a free nation, born of 56 men who signed their name on a document that would essentially mean either freedom or death. Leading up to the signing of the Declaration of Independence, the principles were: Desire, Decision, Faith, Courage, Mastermind, Organized Planning, and most importantly, the Perseverance to keep on in spite of fear and potential death in the cause of creating a free nation.

The above principles are just some that we must master to create a successful organization. Let's face it, business doesn't always go as planned. There is always some type of challenge around the corner. However, having the right systems, structure, culture, processes, and most importantly, having a firm hand on your financials, will provide you a much better edge in navigating the sometimes uncertain climate.

In addition to applying the above principles, get clear on your organization's destination, stay steadfast with your plan, surround yourself with the right mastermind team and you too should be well on your way to *persevering to profits*.

CHAPTER 17:

TO QUALIFY OR NOT TO QUALIFY

"We the willing, led by the unknowing, are doing the impossible for the ungrateful.

We have done so much, with so little, for so long, we are now qualified to do anything, with nothing."

Mother Teresa, Saint

The NFL Combine is where college players get to show off their talent and skills to pro scouts gearing up for the draft. In the 2000 NFL Combine, there was one particular player who placed dead last based on his statistics. He actually ran the slowest 40-yard dash of any player in his position ever.

That particular player was drafted in the fourth round that same year. In week two of the following season, he replaced the number one quarterback who was knocked out of the game. Since that day (as of 2021), this quarterback has played 21 seasons as a starter, has been to nine Super Bowls, winning seven of them, has been the Super Bowl MVP five times, has more playoff wins than any player in the history of the NFL and is now considered the G.O.A.T. greatest of all time. Yes, we're talking about Tom Brady of the New England Patriots, and the Tampa Bay Buccaneers.

Whether you follow football or not, like Tom Brady or not, it simply doesn't matter. I share this because in the creation of a successful organization and when you're hiring your dream team, understand that they actually do not get hired or fired. They either qualify for a position or they don't. Tom Brady qualified himself for the quarterback position and has never relinquished that position since.

When an organization is clear on its culture, it will be clear on who fits in and who does not. When you are looking to create your dream team, you want to look for certain attributes in these individuals. You want to find personnel that are running on all 16 cylinders. It's these individuals that you need to create a high-performance team.

These 16 cylinders are formulated with four components being of Mind, Body, Heart and Spirit. However, they are not all equal in their percentage. Both mind and body of which you will read on a résumé consist of three cylinders each, for a total of six. That leaves 10 cylinders to equal the full 16. Heart and spirit equal the other 10 cylinders, each counting for five. What does this mean? The heart and spirit are the attributes that tell you whether the person has the drive, the passion, and the get-up and go for the position.

At the same time, you also need a leader running on those 16 cylinders. When you have this combination with those who have qualified for their positions by these standards, you will begin to have your high-performance team.

If Tom Brady was judged on mind and body alone back in 2000, he may have never been in the NFL at all, it was his heart and spirit that first drove him to the top.

When you find the right people with heart and spirit, with the passion to learn and do their best, you will certainly be able to teach them the skills to perform. However, if you hire based on résumé alone and leave out the heart and spirit, you will find yourself with an organization not running on all cylinders. And if your organization is not running on all 16 cylinders, you just may never qualify for the bright lights in the big game of business.

CHAPTER 18:

RESISTING YOUR RESULTS

"There are no secrets to success. It is the result of preparation, hard work and learning from failure."

Colin Powell, Retired Four-Star General

The one thing in this world that affects us all in both business and life is that we are always facing a constant state of change. To stay competitive, we must consistently grow and adapt to this change. If we don't, the world may simply leave us behind.

The definition of insanity is "doing the same things over and over again and expecting different results." This theory simply doesn't work. The only way to consistently grow is to stretch beyond your comfort zone, to do things that you haven't done before. You have to do these things that may be uncomfortable for you, yet you must still persevere through these feelings of uncomfortableness. You must measure the results of these new habits and actions. Because as you push through, take action, measure, and begin to realize these new results is when you will actually gain momentum and confidence to go even further and strive harder than ever.

Let's face it, at the end of the day RESULTS is what you are looking to achieve. But the moment you become resistant to change, there are many results that you may never capture, thus limiting your ability to reach the highest levels of success.

The definition of Resistance is *the refusal to accept or comply with something.*

Everyone has their blind spots. If you fail to recognize and address these blind spots you will never grow. Coaching is a very interesting profession as we are always dealing with people's blind spots, including our own, which is why we also have coaches to help us along. Those of us who are open to first getting clear – then learning, adapting, and making the shifts to address these blind spots – are those who will grow, move forward, and achieve better results.

Unfortunately, some are resistant to change, feedback, facing tough questions, or taking constructive criticism. Some simply don't want to recognize or address the blind spots because they may not like what they see. There's an old cliché, "The truth will set you free." So how can you possibly address an issue if you don't know what it is?

Some may actually feel that they already know enough so they resist any potential new learnings. The words "I know" could potentially be the two most dangerous words or thoughts in the human language. While thinking or saying it, you are shutting down whatever potential knowledge that is available to you. There is a vast world of information and knowledge available in this universe. If you are shutting yourself out of this universal equation, you may be shorting yourself out of potential extraordinary results.

There's a great saying by a Navy Seal, "I faced the enemy and the enemy was me." Basically, what this means is what we fear most is what we will resist, and resisting what we fear most may actually block us from achieving what we really want.

The best way to grow beyond this resistance is to take on a coach, one that will help push you through both your comfort zone as well as your resistance zone. When you decide to open up, take down the resistance, drop the "I know," ask more questions, and engage in empowering conversations, you will slowly begin to stretch and grow outside your comfort zone. And most importantly, you just may capture those extraordinary results that have been eluding you all this time.

CHAPTER 19:

SYSTEMATIZATION EQUALS SUCCESS

"Science is the pursuit of pure truth, and the systematizing of it."

P. T. Barnum, American Showman

In the creation of a successful organization, your organization simply must be systematized. Systems are the glue that holds an organization together. Systems are also an essential component of what creates the synergy in a business that we are all after.

If a business or organization doesn't have systems in place, I guarantee that there will be breakdowns and miscommunications. The owner or leader of the organization will also be working way too hard because of this lack of systematization. In addition, if the business is to be sold one day it may never receive its full asking price because of this absence of systematization.

Systems are simply about documenting and delivering consistent repeatable results time after time. You may want to write this down: Systems stands for *Saving Yourself Stress Time Energy and Money! ***Remember this was mentioned earlier****

By asking yourself the question: Is this *Saving Me Stress Time Energy and Money* or is this *Costing Me Stress Time Energy and Money?* This process alone will slow you down long enough to think clearly of what needs to be in place and provide you the proper direction on what to do next.

Take inventory of yourself and/or your business by addressing the following questions. Where in your business are you finding or experiencing the most frustration or bottlenecks that are most impacting your business negatively?

What is the absence of systems in your business that is most negatively impacting your bottom line? Take a moment and write them down. This is important as the lack of systems in an organization is definitely impacting the margins in a negative way.

Are you lacking systems in your – Marketing – Planning – Sales Process – Employee Hiring – Training – Management? Rate yourself on a scale of 1-10. Then ask yourself why you gave yourself that score.

Are your systems up to date? Are they documented clearly and easy to use? How consistently are you in following them? Are you also holding your team accountable for following them?

As you take inventory of any lack of systematization, what's the dollar value related to this lack? How much money is being left on the table over a year period?

Answering these above questions could just be the exercise that takes you, your team, and your organization to a whole new level.

If you are holding yourself to a high level of systematization – congratulations! If you are not holding yourself to these high levels, you and your team are simply working too hard. And if you're working too hard, your business just won't have the opportunity to run at full capacity.

In addition, for smaller business owners, I urge you to not use the excuse of not having enough time to put that system in place. Just think of the stress, time, energy, and money it has already cost by not having these systems in the first place. Remember, your goal is not to work as hard as you can. Your goal is to fully systematize your business to utilize it to make money and provide the quality of life you dream of.

CHAPTER 20:

YOUR TEAM AND THEIR ORGANIZATIONAL TRIDENT

"Coming together is a beginning; Keeping together is progress; Working together is success."

Henry Ford, Founder of Ford Motor Company

When I think of a team, I think of the Navy Seals. They are the ultimate example of how teams are defined. They are united. They hold themselves and their teammates to a very high level of accountability. They never make it about themselves as they always make it about the man next to them and the mission. They are always clear on their outcome and they will execute that mission as quickly and efficiently as possible.

So, when you think of your team, staff, or employees, what image and thoughts do you have of them? Are you proud of every one of them as both individuals and as a unit?

The word TEAM stands for *Together Everyone Achieves More!*

If you are an owner of a company, your one job is to take care of the team. If your team is well trained, educated, motivated, paid on time, held accountable, and recognized for their hard work, they will break down walls for you. Take care of your team and they will take care of your customers; your customers will be happy and come back again and again and refer their friends. This, in turn, will grow your business which is the reason that you started it in the first place.

When things aren't going exactly like you wish, step up as a leader, make it about your team, and things will soon improve.

I leave you with a few of my favorite lines from the Navy Seals Creed to get you thinking about what it takes to build the dream team you want.

- The lives of my teammates and the success of the mission depend on me.

- If knocked down, I will get back up, every time.

- **Focus on results.** Embrace that results are what we're all really after. Commit to delivering like you wish others would do for you.

- **Make lessons of failures**. Minimize the tendency to make a mistake anything more than a lesson on how not to do something. Learn from your experiences and accept them as tuition for future success.

- **Continue on.** Smarter.

- **Reinforce.** Support each other (and ourselves) by continually reminding and encouraging one another to deliver on these points.

- In the worst of conditions, the legacy of my teammates steadies my resolve and silently guides my every deed.

- By wearing the Trident, I accept the responsibility of my chosen profession and way of life. It is a privilege that I must earn every day.

What if all organizations had a Trident for their work, for their team, for their mission – something that says they truly accept the responsibility for their chosen profession? Most importantly, what would be the value and return if they consistently followed through on executing it?

Something to think about…You up for it?

CHAPTER 21:

UNIQUENESS – STAND ABOVE THE PACK

"What sets you apart can sometimes feel like a burden and it's not. And a lot of the time, it's what makes you great."

Emma Stone, Actress

How do you stand on top of the heap compared to all your competitors? What does your company have in place to impress prospective customers with the added value they can expect when they establish a relationship with you? Does your company possess a specific feature so unique that it will stand out as a persuasive reason for someone to deal with you? Is your company simply blending in with the crowd or standing out as a known go-to source in your industry? Understand that if your company's name or slogan is not slipping off the tip of someone's tongue when one is searching for a company in your chosen field – well you have a little more work to do on developing your uniqueness and brand.

Have you ever given any consideration to your company's uniqueness? What's the one trait that separates you from your competition? If everything else is equal when trying to decide which product or service to buy, what dominant uniqueness does your company represent that becomes the difference between winning and losing potential business?

Let's first explore exactly how we would create our uniqueness.

The first exercise would be to go through the process of creating a unique selling proposition (USP). A unique selling proposition (USP) is a well thought out statement that will help your company distinguish itself from other businesses in its industry. In the developing of a USP, you would focus on features or benefits that solve a problem, satisfy a need or take away the customers' pain or concerns. The interesting thing about creating a USP is that this unique attribute or feature doesn't necessarily have to be unique to you, your product, or your services; you only have to create the perception that it is unique in the mind of the audience in your marketplace.

In order to articulate your uniqueness to the customer base in a memorable way, some companies will create taglines or summaries of their USP and insert them into their advertising messages. For example, BMW is *"The ultimate driving experience,"* Fed Ex is *"When your package absolutely, positively has to get there overnight,"* and *"You're in good hands with Allstate."* These slogans are all ingrained in our brain when we think of these companies. This is standing out, this is uniqueness.

This concept of a unique selling proposition (USP) is an important lesson to consider when putting together a marketing strategy. Once you find it, then all you have to do is communicate it to your ideal market.

In developing a marketing strategy that will be used as the foundation of your USP, listed below are a few questions that you should consider from our USP Questionnaire that our clients actually run through to define their own Unique Selling Proposition.

What actually makes me unique? How does my company stand out?

Who are my biggest competitors? What do they do well? What do they do poorly? What is "unique" about them?

In your Ideal Scenario, what is the one thing that if you could guarantee it would make you the market leader?

When identifying your Marketplace, what is most important to an average customer in your industry?

What are the reasons your customers would come to you rather than your competitors?

What three things are your best customers saying about you?

If you could easily overcome any two of your customers' frustrations, what would they be, and how would you overcome them?

Getting clear on these answers, as well as many other questions, will get you well on your way to understanding where you place in your niche in addition to creating a compelling Unique Selling Proposition. Understand that the importance is in the objective to create your uniqueness in standing out amongst your competition while always being on tip-of-tongue by your loyal raving fans.

CHAPTER 22:

VISION CREATES VICTORY

"The great victory of success is being true to the grandest vision of your biggest life."

Robin Sharma, Author

There is a certain recipe or path that you must follow to achieve success. The most important path is called the Six Steps to Success. These six steps must be followed, applied and mastered in order to become successful in any business or organization.

Mastery is the foundation of any business. Mastery consists of four components: Money Mastery – knowing your numbers; Time Mastery – being efficient and intentional with your time; Delivery Mastery – delivering your products and services with consistency; and Destination Mastery – knowing where you are going with your organization. This is where the Vision of your organization comes into play. Your Vision is simply the purpose and overall direction in which your organization is heading. It's like plugging the location into your GPS that creates the big picture to follow.

The following steps are in order of: Niche, Leverage, Team, Synergy, and Results. Results are your end victory where you sell it, replicate it, franchise it, take it public, or whatever your vision of the organization was in the beginning.

As an owner of a business, a leader of an organization, or a coach of a sports team, there always has to be a created vision of where you're going. With a clear vision properly articulated to your team, you will be able to create an energetic and passionate group that will be willing to compete every day on every play.

Why is this important? This is important because before you can ever get any organization excelling to the pace that you want it to go, you first have to be clear on your vision of where you want it to go. When you and the entire team are clear and enrolled in the vision and direction of the company, everyone will bring that extra bit of energy and ownership to the equation each and every day. On the flip side, if your organization does not have a clear vision, it and your team will most likely just float from day to day.

In any organization when you begin the process of strategic planning, visioning should always come first. When visioning the change, ask yourself: What is our preferred future? And be sure to:

- Draw on the beliefs, mission, purpose, and culture of the organization.

- Describe what you want to see in the future.

- Be specific to the organizational outcome.

- Be positive and inspiring.

- Be open to dramatic modifications to the current organization, methodology, teaching techniques, facilities, etc.

KEY COMPONENTS FOR YOUR VISION

Incorporate Your Beliefs

Your vision must be encompassed by your beliefs.

- Your beliefs must meet your organizational goals as well as community goals.

- Your beliefs are a statement of your values.

- Your beliefs are a public/visible declaration of your expected outcomes.

- Your beliefs must be precise and practical.

- Your beliefs will guide the actions of all involved.

- Your beliefs reflect the knowledge, philosophy, and actions of all.

- Your beliefs are a key component of strategic planning.

Benefits of Visioning

The process and outcomes of visioning may seem vague and superfluous. However, the long-term benefits can be substantial. The benefits of visioning:

- Breaks you out of boundary thinking.

- Provides continuity and avoids the stutter effect of planning fits and starts.

- Identifies direction and purpose.

- Promotes interest and commitment.

- Promotes laser-like focus.

- Encourages openness to unique and creative solutions.

- Encourages and builds confidence.

- Builds loyalty through involvement (ownership).

- Results in efficiency and productivity.

If you and your organization are clear on your vision and it is being followed by your entire team – congratulations! If not, take some time and give it some heavy thought of what you would really like to create in the direction and vision of your company.

CHAPTER 23:

CREATING A WIN/WIN WITH YOUR WHY

"Find your why and you'll find your way."

John Maxwell, Author and Leadership Expert

I would like to think that everyone wants to be a winner. No matter what sport you participate in it's easy to clarify winning, it's simply about the final score up on the board. In business, it comes from reviewing your profit-loss statements and your balance sheet. What results are you producing? Are you consistently increasing your top and bottom line?

Whether in sports, business, or life, what does it really take to win? What does it take to consistently stand out as one of the best? What does it take to never lose that mojo that keeps you in the game? I believe the ingredient is that when you compete, you compete against the best *you* that you can possibly be.

In addition to being your best, what actually creates that desire, that internal drive to win? I believe it's about you being clear on your "why." When you are truly clear on your "why," the what and the how will follow.

Nine years ago, I was in a transition phase of moving forward in my coaching practice. However, like many of us who are making a big decision, I needed to go through the process to have the correct answer come to me.

There's a line, "When the student is ready the teacher will appear." I can't tell you how much that phrase resonated with me years back. I say this because about nine years ago I was touched with a stroke of clarity on my "why." That "why" was to serve business owners to get the best out of themselves, their team, and their businesses. It was to have them see more in themselves than they ever thought was possible – to have the confidence to take the action to get them what they really wanted both in business and in life. I knew if I served in this manner, I would be creating a win/win for all involved.

We are all here to serve. It's not necessarily about us. It's about creating wealth and abundance by helping others get what they want. When you come from that place, the results can be astonishing!

When an Olympic athlete hires a coach, he or she hires that coach to help them win the gold, not the silver or the bronze. They hire that coach to help them be 1/100 of a second faster than the other competitors. They hire that coach to help them become the absolute best of the best. However, until they actually make it to the event to compete, *who* are they actually competing against? They are competing against themselves at the absolute best they can be, their own personal best. They are also chasing their "why," the reason they exist.

I had the distinct pleasure of receiving a call from a man who worked for me in the financial industry 25 years ago. It was the first time we've spoken since. He called me to share that I gave him a book where I wrote a note that read, "We are what and where we are today because we first imagined it. Your friend, Michael." He also shared about the success he has created for himself since then and how I gave him the confidence to take that path. He somehow found me on the internet and we work together once again. I am now enjoying the distinct pleasure, honor, and privilege of working with Russ 25 years later on, leading him, his team, and his organization to the next level.

I challenge and encourage you, if you are not already, to get clear on your "why." When you get clear on your "why" and authentically put yourself out there for others, it's absolutely amazing what can happen. I also challenge you to create the path to compete against your best possible you. Because when you venture on this path, following your "why" and being your best you, I guarantee that you'll create a win/win for everyone involved.

CHAPTER 24:

BE EXTRAORDINARY

"The difference between ordinary and extraordinary is a little extra."

Jimmy Johnson, Football Broadcaster, Former Player and Coach

As we migrate towards the end of our Best Business Practices – A through Z of building organizational strength – interestingly enough, I found it a little bit difficult finding the perfect word to represent the letter X. So, I cheated a little and went with eXtraordinary.

The definition of Extraordinary is very unusual or remarkable. The synonyms are: exceptional, amazing, astonishing, astounding, sensational, stunning, incredible, unbelievable, phenomenal, striking, outstanding, momentous, impressive, singular, memorable, unforgettable, unique, noteworthy, out of the ordinary, uncommon, rare, surprising, fantastic, terrific, tremendous, stupendous, awesome and wondrous.

Extraordinary is actually two words in one being extra-ordinary. Warren Buffett has a quote that reads, "It is not necessary to do extraordinary things to get extraordinary results." Being extraordinary is all about doing the little things consistently and relentlessly to achieve extraordinary results.

There's a great little book by Sam Parker and Mac Anderson called *212: The Extra Degree*. In the book, you will read about how 211-degree water is very hot, however, 212-degree water is boiling hot water, hot enough to generate steam, steam able to power a locomotive engine. Huge difference in the outcome, however, only one change in the degree.

The same goes for the difference between an Olympic athlete winning the gold or one winning the silver.

Sometimes it's a 1/100 of a second difference from first to second. But honestly, who remembers any of the silver medal winners? No one.

Take a look at golf championships, horse racing, or auto racing. The difference between first and second place is usually very small, but the difference in the winning purse between first and second is usually very large. Small percentage difference in time, huge difference in earnings.

What does it actually take to be extraordinary? It simply requires a commitment – a mindset to do the necessary little things over and over again until you become extraordinary. It's not an every other day thing – it's an *everyday* thing. It's a standard of excellence to be the best you can be and doing what is necessary to get there.

How do you become extraordinary in business? You have to commit to a standard of excellence in every area of the organization that must also be upheld by everyone involved. Most importantly, you must first create the structure and culture within the organization to achieve this standard of excellence. You need to have the right systems and processes in place for hiring, onboarding with ongoing training.

Creating the culture of accountability and ownership by documenting roles and responsibilities with the entire staff including a follow-up review process. Educating on the proper vital functions for each of your team with KPI's (Key Performance Indicators), using testing and measuring to gauge their results and progress. Having the proper systemized communication measures in place so all are updated and on the same page.

These are just some of the ingredients in creating the structure and culture of an extraordinary organization. Remember the words of Warren Buffett, "It is not necessary to do extraordinary things to get extraordinary results." Extraordinary results are simply about making a commitment to doing the little things consistently and relentlessly to achieve the extraordinary results you desire. Create your systems and processes, pledge your commitment to excellence, and go and be eXtraordinary!

CHAPTER 25:

Y.E.S.!

"If you want to be successful, find out what the price is then pay it!"

Scott Adams, Artist, Dilbert Creator

As we get closer to wrapping up our reading, I believe the perfect word to represent the letter Y is Yes. Why Yes? Because of the word Y.E.S. = *You Expect Success!*

First, please do not be confused with chapter 14 where we discussed being able to say no. That chapter asked the question, "Are you a yes person?" A yes person is someone who says yes to everything and then finds themselves overwhelmed with all they took on. Being a business owner, leader, or just anyone in general, you have to possess the understanding of properly maintaining and managing yourself in knowing that there is a time to say yes and a time to say no. This is one of the key ingredients to maintaining your balance in both business and life.

In this instance, I'm keeping it more personal. I would like to touch on the subject of your state of mind as an entrepreneur, a business owner, leader, manager, or parent. When you are creating your goals, a business plan or just particular assignments that you would like to accomplish, being confident in those plans is the key ingredient to your success in those endeavors. What I am essentially saying is when someone asks you about your confidence in accomplishing those plans or goals, you always want to reply with a strong confident YES! Why? Because saying Y.E.S. programs your conscious and subconscious mind that *You Expect Success!* And when you enter into a venture with the expectation of success, your odds of achieving that goal automatically increases tenfold.

Think about this the next time you are talking to someone about your goals. Listen carefully to the tonality of your voice in how you are expressing confidence, or the lack thereof, in your speaking. Listen clearly as a leader when you are asking someone else about their goals, plans, or assignments. Are they replying with confidence in their voice or do they sound a bit timid in their response? This will give you a clear indication of the potential outcome of these goals, plans, or assignments.

If you are a leader of a team or a parent to children, when they ask for your assistance in a particular area that can help them grow as team members or people, give them a solid YES in your assistance to their questions as you will instill belief and confidence in them.

Understand also, that even though we may actually not be talking out loud in a not so confident manner, our own internal dialogue could still be sabotaging our potential future success.

I'll share a story of how this truly resonated with me. I started my coaching practice in August 2012. On April 9, 2013, my practice had seven full-time clients, it was moving along pretty well. I was attending a regional coaching conference in Orlando, Florida. I had a full calendar of prospect appointments set up for the next 30 days and I felt a big business breakout unfolding on the horizon. I was excitedly ready to mastermind, brainstorm, and plan the following day with dozens of like-minded entrepreneurial coaches. I was ready to rock. The phrase *You Expect Success* was confidently ringing loud in me.

Until the phone rang in my hotel room that evening. My wife called to inform me that one of my brothers had earlier that day committed suicide.

Wow, you talk about a total mindset shift. I distinctly remember lying on the bed staring at the hotel ceiling in disbelief, calling hotlines asking questions to which there were no logical answers. Finally, after a very difficult and unsettled night's sleep, I attended the following day's conference.

Noticing my blank, still in shock stare the following morning, one person asked me if I was OK. I explained what had happened and asked them to keep it quiet as I just wanted to last as long as I could through the day knowing that at some point I would crack, which I eventually did early that afternoon. I just simply wanted to be around positive people as long as I could. I very much didn't want to be alone.

Eventually, I drove home from Orlando and flew to Rhode Island. Now since there is no guidebook on how to deal with this, I thought I would spend time with my family, bury my brother, go back to Florida and continue building my practice. I mean my entire family lives in Rhode Island, I live in Florida. I don't see them often, maybe once a year – anyway, out of sight, out of mind. I thought I could just get back to business as usual.

Wow, was I wrong! Within six months, I was a complete basket case. I have never experienced such a state of spiraling depression in my life. I'm a very positive person, however, I had no idea on how to handle this. I previously lost both my mother and father but nothing could prepare me for something as abrupt and as sudden as this. My emotional state was in major turmoil. My business was now failing, my seven clients had shrunk to one. I was now viewing what I called "my amazing shrinking bank account." Because of my mindset, I was expecting anything but success. My confidence was shot, my energy was wrong, and I wasn't able to be an asset to anyone, most importantly myself.

What turned it around was that I finally reached out to a coach; I expressed a desperate need for assistance. I knew I could no longer ride out this journey alone. We agreed to work together where we worked on me first and my business second. I put in the work. I remember my coach congratulating me for just showing up each day. Slowly but surely, I began my long climb back. Step by step I rebuilt myself and my business up one day at a time to where I once again was producing, and most importantly expecting, success.

The full gratification of this journey came full circle once again in Orlando, in February of 2016 where I received an Action Man Award for Excellence at our North American Conference and had a client up on stage as Young Entrepreneur of the Year. I once again was producing success because I was expecting it.

Henry Ford has many famous quotes, but I will share the one that most rings loud for me. *"If you think you can do a thing or think you can't do a thing, you're right."* Whatever you are most thinking and speaking of is exactly what will be delivered to you.

Consistently be mindful that in any and every conversation you are having, whomever you are having it with, replying with a clear, confident YES will consistently send the message to both yourself and others that *You Expect Success.*

CHAPTER 26:

YOU MUST SLOW DOWN BEFORE YOU CAN ZOOM

"Our subjective experience of time is highly variable. We all know that days can pass like weeks and months can feel like years, and that the opposite can be just as true:

A month or year can zoom by in what feels like no time at all."

Joshua Foer, Journalist

There once was a speedy hare who bragged about how fast he could run. Tired of hearing him boast, Slow and Steady, the tortoise, challenged him to a race. All the animals in the forest gathered to watch. The hare ran down the road for a while and then paused to rest. He looked back at Slow and Steady and cried out, "How do you expect to win this race when you are walking along at your slow, slow pace?"

Hare stretched himself out alongside the road and fell asleep, thinking, "There is plenty of time to relax." Slow and Steady walked and walked. He never, ever stopped until he came to the finish line.

The animals who were watching cheered so loudly for Tortoise, they woke up Hare. The hare stretched and yawned and began to run again, but it was too late. The tortoise was over the line. After that, Hare always reminded himself, "Don't brag about your lightning pace, for Slow and Steady won the race!"

There's no doubt that the world's pace has sped up. If you're a CEO, an executive, a manager, a business owner, or any type of leader, you are most likely strapped with many tasks and responsibilities. Many of us have businesses, teams, families, charities, outside organizations, boards, and activities to contend with. We most importantly have ourselves to take care of. Let's face it, if any of this represents you, you are running.

What's a person to do in this fast-paced environment? Turning to technology isn't the answer as that option has only proved to distract us even more. The answer is simple: slow down to speed up! Yes, slow down to speed up!

If you're a business owner, a leader, a manager, an entrepreneur, or even a parent, you must take the time to slow down. Is it easy to slow down? Heck no! Especially if you're attempting to do it on your own.

If you're challenged in doing it on your own, get someone to assist you. Hire a coach to slow you down. A coach will ask you the right questions, the tough questions, hold you accountable to do what you say you'll do, get you to recognize your blind spots that are holding you back, teach you the techniques, solutions, and strategies to maximize your time and efficiency. With the right coach and proper coaching, you will better yourself, your team, and your company. You will gain clarity and be able to speed up to focus on what's truly important.

I encourage you to take on the challenge of slowing down to speed up! I wrote this book for you, to take this opportunity to slow down, to take a step back, to take a look from the outside in, to become aware of some areas of your life and business that maybe you need to upgrade, shift, or adjust.

I encourage you not to just close this book and put it on the shelf with all the others. Use it as a reference guide to go back to and grade yourself to continually adjust certain areas to improve. When we truly take the time to slow down to see things differently, get clear, create a plan, only then can we speed up and get our organization to *Zoom!*

CHAPTER 27:

CONCLUSION

"Never doubt that a small group of thoughtful, concerned citizens can change the world. Indeed, it is the only thing that ever has."

Margaret Mead, American cultural anthropologist

When I was a new coach, I had the privilege of scheduling a one-hour Skype call with the top coach in our organization. What I learned from that call was you actually at some point have to earn the right to be in the presence of greatness. You have to earn the right to attract great employees. You have to earn the right to attract great customers and clients to continually buy your products and services. You have to earn the right to be respected by others including your spouse and children.

This book has highlighted many areas that we both personally and professionally must tighten up and strengthen to be our best. From taking 100% ownership and responsibility of oneself. To show up each and every day with the right attitude and belief. To consistently invest in ourselves as well as others while understanding the true value of human capital.

We need to avoid procrastination and take action when the right opportunities present themselves. We need to be crystal clear on where we're going and why. When we're clear on that vision, we need to share it with others. We simply need to slow down and be fully present in all our experiences as well as conversations. Most importantly, in business, we need to insert all the right systems, strategies, structures, and solutions so your organization can speed up and run synergistically.

Success is not an accident. Being a great leader is not just a coincidence. It is truly up to us to step up and be our best. I truly believe this is what God most wants and expects of us. True success is not for the faint of heart or for those who are fearful. True success is for the bold. We must strive not for perfection, but for excellence in ourselves and those around us.

My wish for you is to live a fulfilling life of freedom, and independence. To take advantage of everything that is presented on this earth while serving the greater good and having a positive impact on others. To have an organization that truly works for you. I encourage you to work on mastering all of the lessons in this book. Because as you do, you will also earn the right to call yourself "The Master of Knock It Out of the Park Leadership."

SERVICES

KNOCK IT OUT OF THE PARK LEADERSHIP COACHING

Knock It Out of the Park Leadership coaching forces business owners, leaders, CEO's, and entrepreneurs to focus on themselves while devoting the time necessary to systematize and grow their organization and team to achieve significant measurable results. This one-to-one mentor/leadership coaching is not for the faint of heart and is reserved for only those who want to be great and committed to doing the work to get there.

Schedule an appointment with Coach Michael to talk more on how Knock It Out of the Park Leadership coaching can help you. https://calendly.com/coachmichaelcalendar/30-minute-phone

Michael Dill is an authority in the development of business owners, executives, and managers to achieve significant results in their businesses as well as themselves.

Benefits: Personal Growth – Increased Leadership – 100% Accountability – Renewed Passion – Ideal Employee Attraction & Retention – Productivity – Increased Revenue & Profits – Results

GROUP COACHING

The Group Coaching program is designed for smaller businesses that are not quite ready for intense mentorship coaching. The group will consist of two or three small business owners (no two industries alike) that are looking for accountability, systems, and strategies to better streamline their business for growth. The power of this program is the participants interacting and Michael's coaching.

Benefits: Personal & Professional Growth – Increased Confidence – Systematization – Structure – Increased Focus & Time – Increased Revenue & Profits

ALIGNMENT TRAINING/TEAM BUILDING DAY

Alignment Training/Team Building Day is a customized day designed to align, enroll and empower each individual as well as the entire organization. We develop and align with the Vision, Mission and Culture of the organization. We work as a team to improve your effectiveness, communication, behaviors, and ability to influence others to increase productivity and results.

It includes a full day of learning, training, team building exercises, planning, and goal setting to gain clarity and synergy on the future of your organization with all the key members of your team.

Make an appointment with Coach Michael on how I can work with your organization. https://calendly.com/coachmichaelcalendar/30-minute-phone

Benefits: Personal Accountability & Ownership – Increased Initiative & Outlook – Culture – Communication – Retention – Synergy – Action Step Clarity – Results

THINK AND GROW RICH DEEP DIVE

There is no better book written that once fully understood and applied becomes the catalyst to accelerate your own personal wealth and professional growth.

Every year from March through May, Coach Michael takes you through a 12-week deep dive of Napoleon Hill's classic *Think and Grow Rich*. You will learn to fully understand the application of the principles and philosophies of success modeled after the most successful people on the planet at that time.

To learn more or register, go to http://www.businesscoachmichaeldill.com/think-and-grow-rich/

Benefits: Powerful Relationship with Money to set Your Own Income at any Level – Increased Self Belief & Confidence – Clarity – Focus – Wealth Creation & Abundance

To arrange a one-to-one conversation or an in-house workshop, schedule a call with Coach Michael. https://calendly.com/coachmichaelcalendar/30-minute-phone

RECOMMENDED READINGS

Unlimited Power – Anthony Robbins

Think and Grow Rich – Napoleon Hill

Lincoln on Leadership – Donald T. Phillips

The Art of Influence – Chris Widener

Patton on Leadership – Alan Axelrod

212 Leadership – Mac Anderson

George Washington on Leadership – David O. Stewart

Jim Moran The Courtesy Man – Jim Moran

The Success Principles – Jack Canfield

Never Split the Difference – Chris Voss

Outwitting the Devil – Napoleon Hill

The E-Myth Revisited – Michael E. Gerber

Profits Aren't Everything, They're the Only Thing – George Cloutier

The Richest Man in Babylon – George S. Clason

Start with Why – Simon Sinek

Fail-Safe Leadership – Linda Martin & Dr. David G. Mutchler

One Minute Manager – Ken Blanchard

Raving Fans – Ken Blanchard & Sheldon Bowles

How Full Is Your Bucket? – Tom Rath & Donald Clifton

The 4 Disciplines of Execution – Chris McChesney, Sean Covey & Jim Huling

How Successful People Think – John Maxwell

Rich Dad Poor Dad – Robert T. Kiyosaki

Fearless – Eric Blehm

The Four Agreements – Don Miguel Ruiz

ABOUT THE AUTHOR

Michael Dill, known as Coach Michael, is an award-winning certified business coach, professional speaker, and trainer. He is a proud partner of ActionCOACH Business Coaching Franchise and President of Power & Ice Wealth Creation, a strategic leadership company that works with business owners, leaders, teams, and entrepreneurs to both develop a systematized and structured organization while accelerating their mindset, efficiencies, and effectiveness to grow both personally and professionally to achieve extraordinary results. He is the recipient of the ActionCOACH 2016 & 2020 Action Man Award for Excellence and coached the ActionCOACH 2016 Young Entrepreneur of the Year Award winner.

Michael Dill brings more than 40 years of business and entrepreneurial experience in his leadership, team training, and mentoring practice. He has served in the restaurant industry as well as the financial and consulting profession. His years of experience serving in these various industries have molded him in the mastery of developing highly efficient teams.

Since 2012, Michael has coached hundreds of business owners to achieve their goals and take their business to the next level. His clients report a 26% average increase in year over year growth, through improvements in sales, marketing, team development, and efficient systems. His practical business experience coupled with a track record of success make him an invaluable resource for business owners and professionals.

Michael has been married to his lovely wife Susan since August of 1988, and has two grown children, Victoria and Zachary. He is an avid scuba diver and spearfisherman. Enjoys fishing, cooking, painting, staying in shape, along with an occasional scotch and cigar. His juice is simply having a part in others' personal and professional growth.

Coach Michael, 6810 FL-7, Coconut Creek, FL 33073

Phone: (954) 596-0715 and (954) 675-9536

E-mail: michaeldill@actioncoach.com

Website: www.BusinessCoachMichaelDill.com